CW00382102

ON SOLID GROUND

By Kenn Baird

With Dan and Nori Chesney

PUBLISHED BY
MAKE KNOWN MEDIA, Ltd.

Published by Make Known Media

Edited by Jennifer Cupido

Cover Design by Jennifer Cupido and Sarah Dodds

Printed by Europa Print, London, UK

TABLE OF CONTENTS

DEDICATION

This book is dedicated to all who have begun a new journey. By receiving Jesus Christ as Saviour, you have taken the first step. Now your heavenly Father wants you to inherit all that he has promised in his Word, the Bible. This journey will be an adventure like no other. It will be filled with God experiences, trials, successes, impossibilities that suddenly become possibilities, fears that are turned into faith, and questions that lead to new-found wisdom. Your life can be built on solid ground because you now stand on the Rock, Christ Jesus.

Every Christian's walk with God is unique. Even though we have similar beliefs, a common theology, shared values and experiences, the truth is that God relates to us as individuals and our walk reflects the value the Father places in each of us.

This book is written to help you build on solid ground. Just as a builder lays a firm foundation before adding structure to a house, you are building on the solid rock Christ Jesus. Each builder has materials and tools for the job and all must use basic principals to achieve a strong structure. But the individual skills, knowledge, and personality of the builder will have a strong bearing on the way the house turns out. These skills can determine whether or not the house will stand.

So as you begin the task of building your life on the solid ground, our prayer is that the principals in this book will help you construct a life that will last, a life based on the eternal truths of the Word of God, a life that will be successful and strong.

As you read through each chapter, have your Bible close at hand. It is your builder's manual, specifically designed to guide you in your personal building project.   And remember to pray, asking God to give you wisdom for any questions you may have.

Our prayer is that you will grow in grace and wisdom as you build your life on solid ground. We dedicate this book to you.

WHAT IS A CHRISTIAN

By Dan Chesney

Becoming a Christian is a miraculous event. Whether it happens in a quiet moment of decision, or through revelation, or a dynamistic encounter with God, redemption through Christ still produces the same result - a changed life. For some the changes are immediate and dramatic, for others change comes slowly and progressively. However, the proof of our salvation is not in our conversion experience but in our faith in the Son of God. It's what we believe that matters.

Paul writes in Romans 10:9-10, that "...if you confess with your mouth, 'Jesus is Lord,' and believe in your heart that God raised him from the dead, you will be saved. For it is with your heart that you believe and are justified, and it is with your mouth that you confess and are saved."

Notice that Paul says to, "believe in your heart." It is not our intellectual understanding that saves us, it our heart – faith in God's Word. There are millions of people who study the Bible, go to church, say prayers, participate in their congregation, but are not true Christians. They're religious, they're committed, they're knowledgeable, but they are not saved. Why is this? It is because for them it's all head knowledge, not heart – faith. We understand with our minds, but we believe with our heart. That is the difference.

Again Paul explains this in Romans 14:17, "For the kingdom of God is not a matter of eating and drinking, but of righteousness, peace and joy in the Holy Spirit." Paul is making a distinction between the physical and the spiritual, eating and drinking (physical), righteousness, peace and joy (spiritual).

God is always focusing on our hearts, our spirit life. Religion always focuses on the visible, the external. Jesus said in Matthew 18:35, "This is how my heavenly Father will treat each of you unless you forgive your brother from your **heart**." And again in Matthew 22:37, "Jesus replied: 'Love the Lord your God will all your **heart** and with all your soul and with all your mind." Notice that the heart is first. That's because when our hearts are right, than the mind and soul follow. Once we know the Truth, our thinking, character and emotions all become healthier.

When Jesus was teaching on prayer he said in Mark 11:23, "I tell you the truth, if anyone says to this mountain, 'Go, throw yourself into the sea,' and does not doubt in his **heart** but believes that what he says will happen, it will be done for him." Faith is always a heart issue, not an intellectual concept. That's why our salvation is not based on our abilities, our gifting or our IQ. It's based on Ephesians 3:17, "so that Christ may dwell in your hearts **through faith**." We are instructed by the Lord to grow in understanding, wisdom and character, but our foundation will always be faith in Jesus Christ, a faith that springs from the heart. People that are religious can look good, but the question is, are their hearts right. The Pharisees in the Bible were very religious people, but God said this of them in Acts 7:51, "You stiff-necked people, with uncircumcised hearts and ears! You are just like your fathers: You always resist the Holy Spirit." Their outward actions were very pious, but their hearts were far from God.

THE FIRST MIRACLE

This is why the first miracle of salvation is forgiveness. Forgiveness is the door to all of the blessings of God. It's God's first priority, to set us free from all our sins, our guilt and our shame. Acts 26:18 says, "to open their eyes and turn them from darkness to light, and from the power of Satan to God, so that they may receive forgiveness of sins and a place among those who are sanctified by faith in me." And again in Ephesians 1:7, "In him we have redemption through his blood, the forgiveness of sins, in accordance with the riches of God's grace." And

4

how was God able to forgive us? By letting his son Jesus Christ take our place and pay the full price for our sins on the Cross. Romans 3:25 (MB) says, "God sacrificed Jesus on the altar of the world to clear that world of sin. Having faith in him set us in the clear. God decided on this course of action in full view of the public – to set the world in the clear with himself through the sacrifice of Jesus, finally taking car of the sins he had so patiently endured."

Paul again says this in Galatians 1:3 (MB), "Jesus Christ rescued us from this evil world we're in by offering himself as a sacrifice for our sins. God's plan is that we all experience that rescue." By removing the barrier of sins through forgiveness God is able to bring us to himself. This is the great work of Jesus Christ on the cross. We should have died for our sins, but Jesus died in our place, suffering the full consequences of all of our sins. Romans 6:23 says, "For the wages of sin is death, but the gift of God is eternal life in Christ Jesus our Lord." Sin always causes death, and that is why Jesus had to die, because of our sins.

When we accept God's gift of forgiveness through Jesus Christ by faith, we are then free to live in God's presence. Hebrews 10:22 says, "let us draw near to God with a sincere heart in full assurance of faith, having our hearts sprinkled to cleanse us from a guilty conscience and having our bodies washed with pure water." We are no longer separated from God because Jesus has cleared the way. This is the power of forgiveness. And this is why forgiveness is the door to all of God's blessings to us.

The second miracle that takes place at our conversion is we receive a new nature. All of us have a human nature, and that is why humans reproduce humans. Every nature reproduces after it's own kind. Trees reproduce trees, birds reproduce birds and so on. And God reproduces after his own kind as well. 2 Corinthians 5:17 says, "Therefore if anyone is in Christ, he is a new creation: old has gone the new has come!" How does a person become a new creation when they are born again? They receive the very life of God into their spirit man. 1 John 5:11-12 says, "And this is the testimony: God has given to us eternal life, and this life is in his Son. He who has the Son has life: he who does not have the Son of God does not have life." The Barclay translation says, " God gave us eternal life, and that his Son is the source of this life. My purpose in writing this letter to you is to give you the assurance that you do possess eternal life."

How extraordinary, that we would receive the life of God, and in that life is the nature of God. That's why 2 Peter 1:4 (KJV) says, "Whereby are given unto us exceeding great and precious promises: that by these you might be partakers of the divine nature." The New Life translation says, "Through these promises you can have God's own life in you now that you have gotten away from the sinful things of the world which came from wrong desires of the flesh." And the New English Bible says that we "come to share in the very being of God." But my favourite translation of this verse is from J.B. Phillips, which says that we receive "God's own indestructible heredity."

This is why we are new creations, because now we have a new nature, God's nature, and God's life. This does not mean that we are God, but it does mean we share his life. This is why God calls us his children. And this is why Jesus told us to pray in Matthew 6:9, "Our Father in heaven." God is now our Father but we are his true children because through Jesus' death, resurrection, and glorification, he made a way for God to bring us back to him. No wonder Paul wrote in Ephesians 2:4-5, "But because of his great love for us, God, who is rich in mercy, made us alive with Christ even when we were dead in transgressions – it is by grace you have been saved."

What grace, what mercy, what love, that God would not only remove all the negativity of sin, but then he would give us all the blessedness of his life and nature in it's place! Ephesians 2:5 says in the Jordan translation, "...God in his overflowing sympathy and great love breathed the same new life into us as into the Christ." And Romans 8:10 in the Williams translations says, "But if Christ lives in you, although your bodies must die because of sin, your spirits are now enjoying life because of right standing with God."

Now that we are Christians, have this new life and new nature, we have been placed in a new kingdom. We use to live in the kingdom of darkness, but now we are in the kingdom of light, in the kingdom of God. This means we have to learn how to live in this new kingdom, just as you would if you lived in a different country. Our thinking, our behaviour, our values, our goals, our priorities, our whole way of life would need to change. Colossians 1:13 says, " For he has rescued us from the dominion of darkness and brought us into the kingdom of the Son he loves."

When we were not Christians we thought like everybody else. We did as everybody else did. But now we need to learn how to live the way God wants us to live. Ephesians 2:1-3 says, "As for you, you were dead in your transgressions and sins, in which you used to live when you followed the ways of this world and of the ruler of the kingdom of the air, the spirit who is now at work in those who are disobedient. All of us also lived among them at one time, gratifying the cravings of our sinful nature and following its desires and thoughts. Like the rest, we were by nature objects of wrath." Now Jesus is calling us to follow him, to learn his ways, think as he thinks, to act as he acts because we now have his nature.

This is what it means to be a follower of Jesus, to be like Jesus, to be a Christian. And this is the third miracle of becoming a Christian: We reflect God's glory on earth. There are many people who call themselves Christians, but their speech, behaviour, attitude, and priorities do not reflect the nature of Christ. It's like meeting someone who says they are a football player. How exciting! You would naturally ask them what team they play for? You wouldn't expect that person to say, "Well, I don't really play on any particular team. But I know the names of all the players on Manchester United. I know all their statistics, where there games are going to be held, I know their salaries and who they're married to." After listening to them you would conclude that they're not a football player but a fan. And so it is with many people who call themselves Christians. They might know the Bible, go to church and say the right things, but does their life truly reflect the nature of Jesus Christ? That is the true test.

Paul was addressing this very issue in Ephesians 4:17-24, "So, I tell you this, and insist on it in the Lord, that you must no longer live as the Gentiles do, in the futility of their thinking. They are darkened in their understanding and separated from the life of God because of the ignorance that is in them due to the hardening of their hearts. Having lost all sensitivity, they have given themselves over to sensuality so as to indulge in every kind of impurity, with continual lust for more. You, however, did not come to know Christ that way. Surely you heard of him and were taught in him in accordance with the truth that is in Jesus. You were taught, with regard to your former way of life, to put off your old self, which is being corrupted by its deceitful desires; and to put on the new self, created to be like God in true righteousness and holiness."

Now we have to put on this new nature of righteousness and holiness. But how do we do that? It's simple - by prayer, spending time in the Word of God and being faithful to attend a local church regularly. We already have a new nature, which is righteous and holy, but now we have to **act** righteous and holy, and that is a lifelong pursuit. Just as a human baby has everything already in their genes, it will take a lifetime to reach the baby's full potential. What shapes a person throughout life is the relationships they form with others.

Spending time with other people shapes us as Christians. This is why we need to spend our time with Jesus, so that he becomes our greatest influencer. We cannot be a follower of Jesus and follow everything else at the same time. No, there is only one way. The very meaning of the word Christian is 'Christ like'. This is now our destiny, our purpose, and our call, to shine the light of Christ to all of those in darkness around us. Jesus said in Matthew 10:38-39 in the Message Bible, "If you don't go all the way with me, through thick and thin, you don't deserve me. If your first concern is to look after yourself, you'll never find yourself. But if you forget about yourself and look to me, you'll find both yourself and me."

For a Christian, there is no other way but through Jesus, as he said in John 14:6, "I am the way, the truth and the life, no one comes to the Father but by me." And again in Matthew 6:33, "But seek first his kingdom and his righteousness, and all these things will be given to you as well." Jesus is the first and last of our lives, he is our all in all. And as we give ourselves to Jesus, he will give his all to us, blessing upon blessing, beyond all that we can imagine. It is a life of miracles!

BELONGING TO GOD'S FAMILY

By Kenn Baird

When we place our faith in Christ, God becomes our Father, we become his children, other believers become our brothers and sisters, and the church becomes our spiritual family. This incredible family of God includes all believers in the past, in the present, and all who will believe in the future. Whilst it is true that God created everyone, it is just as true that not everyone belongs to God's family. We can only be a part of God's family by being born again. You became part of a human family by your natural birth but you become a member of God's family by your spiritual birth.

Everyone is important. God believes that and so do I. If you were to visit our home a plaque hanging in our entry hall would immediately confront you. It reads, 'With family, everyone is important and none get left behind'. For Kath and I, that is not just a nice phrase adorning a space on our wall. That is a principal by which we live.

Enthusiasm is contagious. It is very difficult to remain neutral or indifferent in the presence of a positive mindset. Now turn to Philippians 4:8 in your Bible. Can you see my point? Just like our earthly family, each person in God's family is important (Ephesians 4:14-16).

There is a second plaque in our home that we hold in equal regard. This time you only see it as you come down the stairs and prepare to leave the house. It reads, "As for me and my house, we will serve the

Lord" (Joshua 24:15 NKJ). Because we belong to God's family, we desire to serve the Lord and not the other way around. We are not serving God to attempt to earn a place in his family. God has accepted us. None of us deserve that acceptance but because of what Jesus has done we are accepted. That's good news!

Sadly however, many people never learn to appreciate this incredible truth of being accepted into God's family. Imagine if I knew you had a need and £100 would completely cover the need and change your life. The trouble is that you do not have £100 nor do you have any access to gaining it from any source. I come along and place into your hands the very sum you desperately need. You are overjoyed and amazed, I am thrilled at being able to help, and it is a great moment for both of us.

Then everything changes - as I walk away I hear you speak the ten words that break my heart. You say, "I will pay you back as soon as I can." You see, I gave you a gift but you turned it into a debt. I set you free but you placed yourself back into bondage.

That's what many people do with God's incredible gift of belonging to his family. We act as if we need to repay the gift, as if our belonging depends on our earning it. Listen carefully. It is a gift, which is a part of your salvation, and it cannot be earned. Let that great truth wash over you. Take it on board and start living in its reality. Followers of Jesus have a special relationship to God. We are a part of God's family, and people outside of Christ cannot experience this special family relationship (2 Corinthians 6:14-18).

One of my favourite stories is the story of the microwave. A man sent his parents a new microwave oven as a Christmas gift. This was their first microwave and they were excited to become part of the 'instant generation'. The box was unpacked and the microwave plugged in. Then literally within seconds, the microwave transformed two smiles into frowns! Even after reading the instructions, they couldn't make it work.

Two days later, the mother was having coffee with a friend and confessed her inability to get the microwave to even boil water. "To get this silly thing to work", she exclaimed, "I really don't need better instructions. I just need my son to come along with the gift!"

When God gave the gift of salvation, he didn't send a booklet of complicated instructions for us to figure out. He sent his Son.

Now here is the good news. God gave us the incredible gift of salvation, the amazing gift of prayer and the astoundingly beautiful gift of his Holy Spirit. In addition to all of that, as if we are not blessed beyond belief already, he also gives us the privilege of belonging to his family.

The moment you were spiritually born into God's family, you were given some astounding birthday gifts: the family name, the family likeness, family privileges, family intimate access, and the family inheritance (1 John 3:1, Romans 8:29, Galatians 4:6-7, Romans 5:2, 1 Corinthians 3:23, Ephesians 3:12, 1 Peter 1:3-5, Romans 8:17).

There is a great difference between effectiveness and efficiency. Efficiency is doing things right but effectiveness is doing the right thing. When God allows us to become part of his family, he is enabling us to receive a great gift. It is therefore important for us to understand how to receive his gift. Here is another story to illustrate this point.

There was a little old lady who was nearly blind. She had three sons who each wanted to prove he was the best. The first son bought her a 15-room mansion, thinking this would surely be the best that any of them could offer her. Her second son bought her a beautiful Mercedes with a chauffeur included, thinking this would surely win her approval. Her youngest son realized he had to do something even better, so he brought her a parrot he had been training for 15 years to memorize the entire Bible. She could ask the parrot any verse in the Bible, and he could quote it word for word. What a gift that would be!

The old lady went to the first son and said, "Son, the house is just gorgeous, but it's really much too big for me. I only live in one room so this house of yours is too large to take care of and clean. I really don't need the house, but thank you anyway."

She then confronted her second son. "The car is beautiful," she said. "It has everything I could ever want on it but I don't drive and really don't like the chauffeur, so please return the car."

She went to her third boy and said, "Son, I just want to thank you for your most thoughtful gift. That chicken was delicious!"

And that is all too often how we misunderstand the gifts of God. The invitation to be part of God's family is universal.

Look at these verses in your Bible and note the connections between them: Mark 8:34, Acts 2:21, Romans 10:13, 2 Peter 3:9. Did you notice that there is one condition in each passage? It is faith in Jesus Christ.

Not only are we born again into God's family through faith, but God also adopts us as his children and heirs, (Romans 8:15, 23, Galatians 4:5, Ephesians 1:5). We don't deserve to be God's children but he has adopted us because he loves us. Oswald Smith in his wonderful book _The Man God Uses_ [1] talks of a fourfold need for the new Christian's life. In fact, I believe that every Christian regardless of their spiritual age should read this book. Smith (who himself became a follower of Jesus in 1906) highlights the connection between the natural infant and spiritual infant's needs.

The Need for Food: Correct diet is essential for a healthy baby's growth and so it is with you. Your church should provide you with a healthy, balanced, spiritual diet of God's word.

The Need for Fellowship: Growing children must learn to express themselves to make their needs known. That is true for you also. Learn to talk to God in prayer. But, also learn to relate with your brothers and sisters in your new spiritual family.

The Need for Exercise: A growing child must exercise to grow strong. Likewise a growing follower of Jesus must learn to exercise their new faith in every area of life.

---

[1] Oswald Smith, _The Man God Uses_, Lakeland 1983

The Need for a Proper Atmosphere: Temperature is everything for new babies and so it is with new babies in Christ. If you are surrounded by cold religious formality then you will spiritually freeze up. If you are surrounded by excessive heat (all hot air and hard to breathe) then you will be uncomfortable. Make sure you are in the right place.

So take care of your new life. Feed it, give it fellowship, exercise it, and make sure the atmosphere is right. Do this and you will grow. That's exactly where your new spiritual family plays its part. Experience is not what happens to a person but rather what that person does with what happens.

Now read 1 John 5:4 in your Bible. From this passage we understand that our spiritual family will last forever. Our families on earth are wonderful gifts from God, but they are temporary and fragile, often broken by divorce, distance, age and inevitably, bereavement. On the other hand our relationship to other believers will continue throughout eternity. It is a much stronger union, a more permanent bond than blood relationships.

God created a need to belong in us so that we would desire to belong to him and to be part of the family of God. Coming to Christ is not the only step necessary for receiving the wholeness and healing that only Jesus can give. Accepting the fact that you belong to Christ and are fully loved and appreciated, valued, and counted as worthy by our heavenly Father is an act of faith and receiving that is quite separate from accepting Jesus.

Believing that God accepts us is tremendously important. Remember, God knew before you were born that there would be difficult times in your life when others would reject you. He knew there would be times when your faith would cause you to be persecuted, rejected, or mocked. Jesus knows how rejection feels. At his arrest his followers fled. Peter, one of his closest disciples, denied knowing him three times. As Jesus was dying on the cross he cried out to his Father, "My God, my God, why have you forsaken me?" (Matt 27:46). He felt the awful isolation of the cross. As the full weight of the sins of all mankind fell upon Jesus, he experienced for the first and only time in history a separation from his Father and the Holy Spirit. Jesus had

13

never known a moment of separation from God nor had he ever known a moment of feeling unacceptable to God. To feel that lack of acceptance was agony for Jesus. And it's agony for us. No need cuts quite as deep as our need to belong, especially our need to belong to our Creator, our heavenly Father. God truly understands the need to belong.

Here is a story that helps us grasp this truth. There was once a farmer who didn't believe in Jesus Christ or the spiritual meaning of Christmas. His wife was a devout believer, and one snowy Christmas Eve she was taking the children to the Christmas Eve service at church. She invited her husband to come with them but he firmly refused. After they left, the winds grew stronger and the snow turned into a blizzard. As the farmer looked out the window, all he saw was a blinding snowstorm. He sat down to relax before the fire for the evening.

Suddenly the man heard the sounds of a flock of birds. When he looked out he saw a large number of birds that had been disoriented by the storm. The farmer had compassion for them and wanted to help them. He thought to himself, "The barn would be a great place for them to stay! It's warm and safe. Surely they could survive the storm there." Soon he was frantically running after the birds trying to chase them toward the barn. The frantic birds just scattered in every direction except toward the barn.

Totally frustrated, the farmer exclaimed, "Why don't they follow me! Can't they see this is the only place where they can survive the storm!"? He thought, "How can I possibly get them into the one place that's safe? If only I could be like one of them I could save them."

He stood silently for a moment as his own words reverberated back to him in his mind: "If only I could become like one of them, then I could save them." His heart became quiet. Then his mind was renewed by the realization. That is exactly what Jesus did! He became one of us to guide us to safety. At last he understood what Christmas was all about. He knew why Christ had come.

As a Pastor I spend a lot of my time talking to people about God. As a Counsellor, I spend a lot of my time listening to people talking about themselves. Basically the common factor is that people desperately crave approval and acceptance. All too often they seek love from those who can never fully provide it for them. This kind of security only comes from Christ.

I once read an opinion poll survey entitled _The Day America Told The Truth_. One of the questions asked by the surveyors was, "What would you be willing to do to obtain $10 million?" A staggering 25% said they would be willing to abandon their families, 23% said they would become prostitutes for a week, and 7% said they would actually murder a stranger. Perhaps the most sobering finding of all was that 91% of those surveyed admitted to having lied regularly both at work and at home. This must surely start your alarm bells ringing.

Pensioners, middle-aged men and women, young adults and teenagers are all caught up in the search for love. Then there is the person who joins committee after committee, becoming so active that they neglect their own family as well as their personal devotional time with the Lord. And let's not forget the person who feels driven to say 'Yes' to every work or social commitment. We mistakenly equate needless and misguided busyness with fulfillment and belonging.

We can all spend a great deal of time and energy looking for love, value, worthiness, acceptance, unconditional favour, and approval from others. But God desires that we have a place on this earth where we feel completely secure and accepted. That's the Lord's desire for us in our families. He desires for each person in a family to have a sense of belonging. The Lord also desires his Church to be a place of belonging. Here people with different spiritual gifts and practical talents can find opportunities to be of service to Christ. Together we can work to advance God's kingdom here on earth. The Church is to be a place of loving acceptance, a place where a person can be appreciated for being a child of God. Belonging should be a feeling of caring, serving, and acceptance.

God believes in you. Do you find that hard to accept? Many do. Read Psalm 139:1-14, especially verse 14, where it says you were "fearfully and wonderfully made." God is talking about you! He made you, but if you stay within a mindset of self-doubt, you will never become the person God destined you to be. Let the truth of God's love and acceptance set you free from self-doubt. If you develop an explorer's attitude, then wherever you go you will discover new ideas waiting to be found. Now read in your Bible, Matthew 7:8.

I love my dog and my dog loves me. It's a fact. I have learned lots of spiritual lessons from my dog. Here are some of my favourites:

1) When a loved one comes home, always run to greet them.

2) Take naps and have a good stretch before rising.

3) Romp, run and play daily.

4) Avoid biting, when a simple growl will do.

5) On warm days stop to lie on your back in the grass.

6) When you're happy, dance around and wag your entire body.

7) No matter how often you are scolded, don't buy into the guilt thing. Run right back and make friends.

8) Never pretend to be something you are not.

9) If what you want lies buried, dig until you find it.

10) When someone's having a bad day, be silent, sit close, given them a gentle nuzzle.

My dog loves me and I love my dog. You see, he knows beyond any shadow of a doubt that he belongs in our family and he feels right at home with us, secure, safe, accepted and loved. But as loving as I am to my dog, it is just a very pale expression of the love God has for you.

Father God loves you. He has adopted you into his family. He wants you to feel loved and accepted. He wants you to know that you belong. He wants you to feel right at home within his family, to appreciate and enjoy the family name, likeness, privileges, intimacy and inheritance (1 John 3:1, Romans 8:29, Galatians 4:6-7, Romans 5:2, 1 Corinthians 3:23, Ephesians 3:12, 1 Peter 1:3-5, Romans 8:17).

That's for now as well as for the future. Welcome to the family!

WATER BAPTISM

By Kenn Baird

In the New Testament, Jesus commands his followers, in what we refer to as the Great Commission (Matthew 28:18-20): "All authority in heaven and on earth has been given to me. Therefore go and make disciples of all nations, baptising them in the name of the Father and of the Son and of the Holy Spirit, and teaching them to obey everything I have commanded you."

We can see that the early church practiced water baptism. In fact on the Day of Pentecost the Apostle Peter instructed the great crowd of people to "Repent and be baptised, every one of you, in the name of Jesus Christ for the forgiveness of your sins. And you will receive the gift of the Holy Spirit" (Acts 2:37-38). The continuing story throughout the book of Acts shows that baptism was an integral part of early church life.

It is my purpose in this short teaching to explain to you exactly what happens in water baptism and at a baptismal service.

There is much confusion today as to how and why the Church baptises believers, and some people experience considerable difficulty in letting go of long-held Church traditions. We must never base our beliefs on traditions no matter how sentimental we are towards them. Belief must be placed firmly upon the Lord Jesus Christ and upon His Word.

The New Testament was originally written in the Greek language and the Greek word for 'baptise' means 'to dip or immerse'. All the believers in the New Testament were baptised by immersion in water. Why not check this out for yourself? Here are some verses to examine: Mark 1:10, Acts 8:38-39, Matthew 3:1-6. John the Baptist was baptising at a certain spot in the river Jordan because "there was plenty of water there" (John 3:23).

We can safely conclude that Jesus himself was baptised by immersion. The Bible records that when he was baptised Jesus "he went up out of the water" (Matthew 3:16), and so did the Ethiopian who was baptised by Philip (Acts 8:38-39).

Many people believe that only babies are baptised in water. This is a classic example of how a traditional view or common misunderstanding can get in the way of what the Bible says about a subject. Jesus said that the Church is made up of people, not bricks and mortar. He states clearly that in order to become part of the Church, we must enter through him (John 14:6). "Jesus answered, I am the way, and the truth and the life. No-one comes to the Father except through me."

When a person realises their need to be born again, they respond by acknowledging their sin and accepting God's forgiveness. This is repentance. And baptism always follows repentance. Baptism is an act of obedience that follows conversion. The Bible is clear in its teaching that a person can only be saved from their sins by accepting the free "...gift of life..." that the Lord Jesus offers to all who call upon his name (Romans 6:23). We cannot act for another in this way. It is always a personal relationship between the Lord Jesus Christ and the person who repents for their sins. So the only babies that were baptised in the New Testament were 'babies In Christ', a reference to new believers.

Baptism is an outward sign of an inward change. It is a public witness to the Lordship of Jesus Christ in a person's life. It is a sign of discipleship and commitment, powerfully displaying to the world that Jesus Christ has risen from the dead and that he brings a new start to all who will believe.

When you are baptised, you publicly testify to the reality that your 'Old Life' with all its sin, is buried with Jesus. The water is symbolic of the grave and as you are raised up out of the water, you begin a new life, a fresh start to live for God from now on.

Take a moment and read the following verses for yourself: Romans 6:1-11, Titus 3:5, Acts 22:16, and Colossians 2:12. Remember, baptism always follows conversion. Baptism is an act of obedience that all Christians ought to obey. There is great blessing in obeying God.

We have seen in Matthew 3:13-17 the account of the baptism of Jesus. It is important for you to remember that Jesus was baptised. It is very important to grasp the fact that in all things Jesus is our chief example. He never commands us to do anything he himself had not done. The very first recorded act of Jesus' public ministry was his submission to baptism by the hand of John the Baptist. The Bible records that Jesus "he went up out of the water" (Matthew 3:16). Baptism was and always is by full immersion. Immersion is the only form of baptism that could symbolise death, burial and resurrection (Romans 6:3-11, Colossians 2:12).

As we have seen, Jesus commands all believers to 1) Go 2) Teach 3) Baptise (Matthew 28:19). But before we 'Go' we must also be baptised (Acts 2:38, Acts 10:48). As God's people, we must always make it our aim to obey the Lord because obedience to Jesus is a test of our love for him (John 14:15, John 15:14).

Baptism By Immersion

In Acts 8:26-40 we encounter the story of Philip and the Ethiopian Official. Here we have a clear example of New Testament water baptism. It is an act of identification with Christ. When we become believers, two things occur immediately: 1) Our old life is finished, and 2) our new life has begun. We have died with Jesus to sin and have risen with Jesus to a new life. These great truths are demonstrated by water baptism.

As we enter the water we present our bodies for symbolic burial, dead to our old way of life. Just as Christ died for our sin, so we die to sin in our lives. The water represents the grave where we leave the old life behind. By going under the water we show symbolically that our old life is buried. Just as Christ was buried in the tomb, being lowered under the water puts our life as a sinner out of sight. We then arise up out of the water symbolising resurrection. Just as Jesus rose from the dead, so we rise to a new life in him.

Water baptism for a believer is the biblical expression of a commitment to die to the old way of life and live for God alone. Can you now see how it is a death, burial and resurrection (Romans 6:4, Colossians 2:11-12) to the old nature, the old ways, habits and lifestyle?

That is what water baptism is all about. It is identification with Jesus Christ, recognition that he is now your master and you are his disciple (Matthew 28:19). It means you have decided to commit yourself to obey Jesus Christ. Water baptism is a separation between the old life of disobedience and the new life of obedience through the Holy Spirit.

Think of a time when you posted an important letter to a friend. Once you drop it into the post box you trust that it will safely reach its destination still intact within its protective envelope. That is a good picture of baptism. When we become followers of Jesus, our lives are like that letter travelling towards its destination of Heaven. The letter is safely sealed in the envelope that becomes its secure vehicle of travel for the journey. In the act of water baptism we receive a sealing into our salvation. That is why Christians refer to baptism as 'an outward sign of an inward work'.

What About Infant Baptism or 'Sprinkling'?

It is very important to realize that baptism is not an optional extra to our salvation in Christ, but it is just as vital to remember that baptism is not salvation. Heaven is full of sincere believers who have not been baptised by immersion. A good example of this is the thief on the cross next to Christ (Luke 23:32-43). Always be on your guard against adopting a legalistic viewpoint.

Baptism does not save us. Neither does it make us members of the Church. Both of these occur at the moment of accepting Christ as our Lord and Saviour. But, the Lord nevertheless commands his disciples, in all places through all ages, to be baptised. As followers of Jesus we should be eager to show our love for him through our obedience to him. Jesus clearly states that if we love him, we will obey him (John 14:15) and if we obey him, we are his friends (John 15:14).

But what about 'Sprinkling' rather than full immersion as a form of water baptism? Perhaps the following amusing incident will help clarify the issue.

A father was visiting a local church with three of his young children, including his five-year-old daughter. It was the baptism service of the tiny infant child of a close family friend. As was customary, the father sat in the very front row so that his children could properly witness the service. The little five-year-old girl was taken by this, observing that the minister was saying something and pouring water over the infant's head. With a quizzical look on her face, the little girl turned to her father and asked, "Daddy, why is he brainwashing that baby?"

Now that might bring a smile to your face and let me stress that it is not my intent to offend brothers and sisters in other parts of God's family who might practice infant baptism. The point is this - are you willing to let go of traditions and sentimentality and seriously look at what the Bible instructs?

The only allowance for the break in the immersion formula is found in the oldest authentic Church history document we have – _The Teaching of the Twelve Apostles_ (also called _The Didache_ - a handbook for new Christian converts consisting of instructions derived directly from the teachings of Jesus). Here we read:

"Now about baptism, baptise this way: after first uttering all of these things, baptise 'into the name of the Father and of the son and of the Holy Spirit' in running water. But if you do not have running water, baptise in other water. Now if you are not able to do so in cold water, do it in warm water. Now if you don't have either, pour water three *times on the head, 'into the name of the Father, and of the son, and of the holy Spirit.'"*

This dispensation was given only for conditions where there was a shortage of water (i.e., deserts or drought conditions). It has no bearing on whether or not a building has a baptismal pool.

The Proper Candidates for Baptism

Anyone who has repented of sin and confessed Christ as Lord is a proper candidate for baptism. Infants were never baptised in the scriptures. Infants are considered to be below the age of accountability. In other words, they are unable to understand the need for a saviour. Remember, baptism is an outward sign of an inward change.

Sometimes we read of whole households being baptised. Acts 16:14-15 is one such example. These are clearly members of the family who are able to understand. They are not infants. Again in Acts 18:8 we are introduced to 'Crispus' house. Here we are told that first they believed, and then they were baptised. There it is -- baptism always follows salvation and never the other way around.

The Formula for Baptism (Matthew 28:19)

'Sabellianism' is a heresy that teaches that baptism is only to be in the name of Jesus. It denies the doctrine of the trinity and misquotes verses such as Acts 19:3-5 and Acts 10:48. The biblical expression 'in my name' means 'by my authority' (see Mark 16:17). The formula for baptism is that which Jesus himself gave in Matthew 28:19, "in the name of the Father, and of the Son, and of the Holy Spirit."

Giving our all to Jesus is of vital importance to successful Christian living. After all, Jesus gave his all for us. Read the following story and then jot down the main points as it unfolds in your heart and mind.

The Son and All

Many years ago there was a man who had an only son. Together they shared a love of fine art and travelled the world, adding only the finest treasures to their collection. Priceless works by Picasso, Van Gogh, Monet and many others adorned the walls of the family estate.

As winter approached one year, war engulfed the nation. The young man received his conscription papers and left to serve his country. After a few weeks, his father received a telegram. The young man had died while attempting to rescue a wounded comrade.

Distraught and lonely, the old man faced the upcoming Christmas holidays with dread. What was left to celebrate? His joy was gone. Then early on Christmas morning, a knock on the door awakened the grieving man. As he walked to the door, the masterpieces of art on the walls seemed to mock him. Of what value were they without his son to share their beauty?

Opening the door, he saw a young man in uniform with a large package in his hands. "I was a friend to your son," he said. "As a matter of fact, I was the one he was rescuing when he died. May I come in? I have something to show you."

The soldier told of how much the man's son had talked about art and the joy of collecting masterpieces alongside his father. "I'm no artist myself," the soldier said shyly, "But I wanted you to have this." And he handed the old man a package.

As the old man unwrapped the package, it revealed a portrait of his son. Though the art world would never consider it a work of genius, the painting somehow captured the young man's likeness, albeit simply and clumsily. Overcome with emotion, the man thanked the soldier, promising to hang the picture above his fireplace.

A few hours later the old man set about his task. True to his word, he put the painting above the fireplace, pushing aside a fortune in classic artworks. The old man sat in his chair and spent Christmas day gazing at the gift.

During the days and weeks that followed, the man gradually realized that even though his son was no longer with him, the boy would live on because of those he had touched. His son had rescued dozens of wounded soldiers before a bullet had cut him down.

Fatherly pride and satisfaction began to ease the old man's grief. The painting of his son soon became his most prized possession. He told his neighbours it was the greatest gift he had ever received.

The following spring, the old man passed away. With the famous collector's passing, the art world eagerly anticipated a great auction. According to the collector's will, all of the works would be auctioned on Christmas Day, the day he had received the greatest gift.

The day soon arrived, and art dealers from around the world gathered. Dreams would be fulfilled this day. Many would soon claim, "I have the greatest collection." The auction began, however, with a painting that was not on any museum's list.

It was the simple portrait of a young soldier ... the collector's son.

The auctioneer asked for an opening bid but the room was silent. "Who will open with a bid of one hundred pounds?" he asked. Minutes passed and no one spoke. From the back of the room came a gruff voice, "Who cares about that? It's just a picture of his son." More voices echoed in agreement. "Let's forget about it and move onto the good stuff."

"No," the auctioneer replied. "We have to sell this one first."

Finally, an old man, poorly dressed and obviously without means spoke. "Will you take one pound for the painting? That's all I have. I knew the boy, so I'd like to have it."

"I have one pound," called the auctioneer. "Will anyone go higher?" After more silence, the auctioneer said, "Going once; going twice; sold!" The gavel fell. Cheers filled the room and someone exclaimed, "Now we can get on with it!"

But at that moment, the auctioneer looked up at the audience and quietly announced, "Ladies and Gentlemen, that concludes our auction." Stunned disbelief blanketed the room. Finally someone spoke up. "What do you mean, it's over? We didn't come here for a picture of some old guy's son! What about all these paintings? There are millions of pounds' worth of art here!"

The auctioneer replied, "It's very simple. According to the will of the father, whoever takes the son gets it all".

Take a moment and jot down your thoughts. Jesus commands his followers, believe and be baptised.

So How Does Baptism Happen?

Many churches offer baptism classes for people who want to be baptised. These classes help candidates understand more about the meaning of baptism.

Many church buildings have a baptismal pool at the front of the church that is often hidden under the floor, with steps going down into it. Other churches that do not have a baptismal pool might use a local swimming pool, or even a river or the sea.

During the service, those being baptised will give a testimony to the congregation on how they became a Christian and why they have chosen to be baptised. Then, immediately before baptism, whilst in the water, they will be asked basic questions of commitment, including an acknowledgement of Jesus as Lord and Saviour.

If someone is in a position to disciple another person then they are qualified to baptise that person. However it is always best to submit to the leadership of the church and enquire about the procedure for baptism and how to access the baptism class.

Many churches may also use a baptism service as an evangelistic outreach opportunity in which your witness through baptism can lead to the salvation of family, friends and visitors.

Once you enter the water, the person baptising you will securely hold on to you to ensure you are stable. This can be practiced in advance. He will then say the words, "I baptise you in the name of the Father, of the Son, and of the Holy Spirit", and carefully lower you into the water backwards until you are fully immersed, then raise you back up to a standing position. You can then leave the water. In many churches the leader or Pastor will then lay hands upon you and pray for a filling of God's Holy Spirit in your life.

So in summary, when you become a candidate for baptism, you confess in a public declaration that you believe that Jesus died for your sins and rose again from the grave. Christ's death, burial, and resurrection are now pictured through your own burial in the baptismal waters.

You also bear witness to your personal experience of regeneration through baptism. You are declaring that you have died to your old life and are resurrected with Christ to walk in a new life. Baptism is the door of induction into discipleship.

Finally, here are some notable biblical baptism experiences for you to look up and study.

Acts 2:41 – 3,000 new converts in Jerusalem

Acts 8:12 – Converts at Samaria

Acts 8:13 – Simon the Sorcerer

Acts 8:36-38 – The Ethiopian Official

Acts 9:18 – Saul of Tarsus

Acts 10:47-48 – The household of Cornelius

Acts 16:15 – Lydia and her household

Acts 16:33 – The Philippian Jailor

Acts 18:8 – The Corinthian converts

Acts 19:5 – The Ephesian disciples

Now it's time for you to talk to your leaders about arranging to be baptised.

HOLY SPIRIT BAPTISM

By Dan Chesney

After you become a Christian, there is an entirely new heavenly world to discover -- spiritual riches, an inheritance provided by Jesus Christ, promises and covenants, blessings and treasures. All of these will take a lifetime to unearth. Some of these treasures will be easily recognized while others will take determination to find. Some truth is hidden, buried in the Bible and in the mind of the Holy Spirit. This is why Jesus tells us in Matthew 6:33 to "...seek first his kingdom and his righteousness, and all these things will be given to you as well." This needs to be a permanent mindset and life-long pursuit for every Christian. Paul said in Philippians 3:14, "I press on toward the goal to win the prize for which God has called me heavenward in Christ Jesus."

One of the greatest gifts that our heavenly Father has given to us is the Holy Spirit, which Jesus commands us to receive after we are born again. Jesus said this to his disciples in Acts 1:4-5, "Do not leave Jerusalem, but wait for the gift my Father promised, which you have heard me speak about. For John baptised with water, but in a few days you will be baptised with the Holy Spirit." Now the disciples had already received the Holy Spirit **within them,** but in a few days they were going to receive the Holy Spirit **upon them**. We need to receive the Holy Spirit in this same way to fully pursue our relationship with the Father.

Jesus spent several years teaching about the Holy Spirit and demonstrating how the Holy Spirit works. By the time they received the

Holy Spirit, the disciples were in great expectation – they wanted all that Jesus had for them. After the Holy Spirit came upon them their lives were revolutionised. They went from being carnal Christians to spiritual leaders, from emotionally based to spirit-based, from fearful to bold, from doubters to believers.

Jesus wants us to have this further blessing of the Holy Spirit for added power and successful Christian living. He wants us to receive all that the early disciples received. To help you understand why we should seek this added blessing, let's look at 10 reasons for the baptism of the Holy Spirit and what he will mean to you.

10 Reasons for the Baptism of the Holy Spirit

Reason 1. <u>The baptism of the Holy Spirit is the last thing Jesus talked about.</u> People generally speak of the most important things in their lives when they are about to die or leave, and it was no different for Jesus. There is a story in John 2:1-11 which verifies this. Jesus had just turned water into wine at a wedding, and when the master of ceremony tasted it he said, "Everyone brings out the choice wine first and then the cheaper wine after the guests have had too much to drink; but you have saved the best till now." God's greatest gifts are waiting for us when we receive his Son. This principle applied to Jesus while he was on the earth. He saved the best for last to give to his disciples.

Jesus explained this to his disciples in the upper room just before his crucifixion. In John 16:7 (NKJV) Jesus said, "Nevertheless I tell you the truth. It is to your advantage that I go away; for if I do not go away, the Helper will not come to you; but if I depart, I will send Him to you." What could be of greater value than to have Jesus with you as your teacher and friend? Yet Jesus said it was to their advantage that he leave and send them the Holy Spirit. Why is this? Jesus knew that it was only the Holy Spirit who would be able to help the disciples live and act as Jesus did. Jesus wanted his friends to have this encounter with the Holy Spirit before they entered into ministry, before they started churches, before they began world evangelism. This is how important the Holy Spirit was to Jesus.

Reason 2. <u>The baptism of the Holy Spirit was a vital part of Jesus' ministry.</u> Luke 3:16-17 says, "I [John] baptise you with water. But one more powerful than I will come, the thongs of whose sandals I am not worthy to untie. He will baptise you with the Holy Spirit and with fire." Then Jesus affirmed these words in Acts 1:5 saying, "For John baptised with water, but in a few days you will be baptised with the Holy Spirit." We accept Jesus as our Saviour, our High Priest, our Healer, our King and Lord, our Shepherd, our Apostle, our God, our Deliver, and our Provider. All of these are a part of his ministry to his church, and so is his ministry of baptising us in the Holy Spirit. It is his will and his gift to us, as much as his gifts of peace, righteousness, and love. This is why Jesus said he would baptise his disciples—it was a continuation of his ministry.

Reason 3. <u>It is God's will for all believers</u>. Jesus said in John 7:37-39, "'If anyone is thirsty, let him come to me and drink. Whoever believes in me, as the Scripture has said, streams of living water will flow from within him.' By this he meant the Spirit, whom those who believed in him were later to receive. Up to that time the Spirit had not been given, since Jesus had not yet been glorified." This is referring to the outpouring of the Holy Spirit in Acts 2:4, "All of them were filled with the Holy Spirit and began to speak in other tongues as the Spirit enabled them."

When Peter was explaining this phenomenon to the general public, he said in Acts 2:15-18, "These men are not drunk, as you suppose. It's only nine in the morning! No, this is what was spoken by the prophet Joel: 'In the last days God says, I will pour out My Spirit on **all people.** Your sons and daughters will prophesy, your young men will see visions, your old men will dream dreams. Even on my servants, both men and women, I will pour out my Spirit in those days, and they will prophesy.'" These verses make it clear that what happened to the disciples on the day of Pentecost is for all believers throughout all of history. Later in this same chapter Peter says in verses 38-39, "And you will receive the gift of the Holy Spirit. The promise is for you and your children and for **all** who are far off—for **all** whom the Lord our God will call."

In Acts 6:3 the early church leaders made the baptism of the Holy Spirit a prerequisite for ministering in the church. "Brothers, choose seven men from among you who are known to be full of the Spirit and wisdom." Jesus had been baptised in the Holy Spirit before starting his earthly ministry, all of the apostles and prophets were filled with the Spirit on the day of Pentecost before they started ministry; and so it became a pattern for the New Testament church. Believers everywhere were filled with the Spirit no matter what their role, station, nationality or status. All were filled.

In Acts 8:14-17 we read about people coming to Christ in Samaria. What was the church leadership's first response to these new believers? "When the apostles in Jerusalem heard that Samaria had accepted the word of God, they sent Peter and John to them. When they arrived, they prayed for them that they might receive the Holy Spirit, because the Holy Spirit had not yet come upon any of them; they had simply been baptised into the name of the Lord Jesus. Then Peter and John placed their hands on them, and they received the Holy Spirit." The early church leadership believed it was God's will for all to be filled with the Spirit. It was a high priority. That is why it was their first prayer for these new believers in Samaria.

In the book of Acts, chapter 9, we have the famous story of the conversion of Saul of Tarsus. Saul was a leading Jew who had persecuted Christians. On his way to the city of Damascus he had a powerful encounter with Christ and he became a Christian, changing his name to Paul. After he was saved, the first thing God did was to send a man named Ananias to pray for Paul to be filled with the Holy Spirit. This is another example of God's will and priority.

In Acts 10 we have another account of people being saved and filled with the Holy Spirit at the same time. Peter said in Acts 10:46, "For they heard them speaking in tongues and praising God."

Following this the early church members and leaders went out from Jerusalem preaching the good news. As a result, many new churches and home groups were started. This is all recorded in the book of Acts between chapters 13 and 28, as well as in many of the Epistles. A Spirit-filled leader started every church mentioned in the New Testament and all of the members were Spirit-filled. They believed it was God's will and priority. As a matter of fact, Spirit-filled authors wrote every single book in the New Testament. You cannot separate the New Testament from the baptism of the Holy Spirit. God reveals his will and priority on every page so that we will have confidence it is his will for us too.

Reason 4. Every New Testament church was Spirit-filled, spoke in tongues, and experienced the gifts of the Spirit in their lives. This was the DNA of the church. This was the pattern established by the fathers of the early church so we would follow it.

To the church in Rome, Paul talks about prophesy in Romans 12, and in chapter 15 he reminds Roman Christians of the signs, miracles, and power of the Holy Spirit that accompanied his ministry when he first came to them.

To the church in Corinth, Paul taught extensively on Spirit-filled church behaviour in chapters 12 and 14. To the church in Galatia, Paul describes the miracles God in chapter 3. And to the church in Ephesus, Paul taught them to pray in the Spirit, be strong in the Spirit, and be filled with the Spirit.

In Iconium, Paul and Barnabas said their message was confirmed with miracles, signs, and wonders (Acts 14). In Lystra, Paul healed a man crippled from birth. The church in Antioch had leaders who were teachers and prophets. In Philippi, a church was started because Paul cast out a demon, and then miracles took place while he was prisoner.

On and on the book of Acts tells of people being saved and churches being started because the message they preached was followed by signs, wonders, miracles, and healings, all evidence of the baptism of the Holy Spirit.

Reason 5. The baptism of the Holy Spirit was a sign that all people of all races could be saved. One of the proofs that Jesus was the Messiah, sent by God the Father, was his baptism in the Holy Spirit. John 1:33 says, "I would not have known him, except that the one who sent me to baptise with water told me, 'The man on whom you see the Spirit come down and remain is he who will baptize with the Holy Spirit.'" Then in Acts 2:22 Peter says, "Jesus of Nazareth was a man accredited by God to you **BY** miracles, wonders, and signs, which God did among you through him, as you yourselves know." And again in Acts 10:38 he says, "how God anointed Jesus of Nazareth with the Holy Spirit and power, and how he went around doing good and healing all who were under the power of the devil, because God was with him." His Spirit-filled ministry was evidence that he was who he said he was.

In Acts 10:44-48, a group of Gentiles came to faith, but the proof that convinced Peter and the other Christians with him that they were genuine was that they also received the baptism of the Holy Spirit. Peter said in verse 47, "Can anyone keep these people from being baptised with water? They have received the Holy Spirit **just as we have**." How did they know that they had received the Holy Spirit **just as the original 120 had**? They knew by what they saw and heard. Their behaviour and speech were similar. As a result of this event, the fathers of the faith all agreed that salvation and the baptism of the Holy Spirit were for all people of all races. Theological history was forever changed.

The writer of Hebrews also confirmed this when he wrote in chapter 2:3-4, "This salvation, which was first announced by the Lord, was confirmed to us by those who heard him. God also **testified to it by signs, wonders and various miracles, and gifts of the Holy Spirit distributed according to His will.**"

Reason 6. The baptism of the Holy Spirit empowers Christians to witness. This was one of the main reasons Jesus commanded his disciples to wait until they had received the Holy Spirit. He knew that they needed supernatural power to live the Christian life as well as change people's lives through their ministry. Jesus was clear. He did not want the disciples to begin their ministry until they had been baptised in the Holy Spirit.

Acts 1:8 says, "But you will receive power when the Holy Spirit comes on you; and you will be my witnesses in Jerusalem, and in all Judea and Samaria, and to the ends of the earth." This is why the book of Acts reads like the Gospels, because the same power that Jesus received is the same power that the disciples received, and the same results followed. They became effective witnesses.

We may not have the same ministry as the first disciples, but we can have the same Spirit to live a victorious life and reach people with the same transforming power. It was said of them that they turned the world upside down. They did this by the power of the Holy Spirit. They were effective witnesses because the world saw Jesus in them through the work of the Holy Spirit.

Reason 7. <u>The baptism of the Holy Spirit releases all the rest of the gifts of the Holy Spirit.</u> The baptism of the Spirit is the door into the supernatural realm of God. Jesus never did one miracle, sign, or wonder until he was first baptised in the Holy Spirit. All of the miracles, signs, wonders, and healings in the book of Acts all followed the outpouring of the Holy Spirit in the second chapter. And throughout history, every revival, every move of God, every outbreak of healings or miracles followed people who were first filled with the Holy Spirit.

In Acts chapter 2, after the disciples were filled with the Holy Spirit, 3000 people were saved, they all spoke in other tongues, and many wonders and miraculous signs were done. In Act 3, a crippled man was healed. In Act 5 the apostles performed many miraculous signs and wonders, so that people were even being healed as Peter's shadow fell on them. In Acts 6 a Spirit-filled man named Stephen performed more great wonders and miraculous signs. In Acts 8 Phillip, a Spirit-filled believer, did miraculous signs, cast out demons, and brought many to Christ. Then when the other apostles came down to see what was happening, the first thing they did was pray for all of the people that had become Christians to be filled with the Spirit. And almost every page after Acts 8 is filled with miracles, healings, deliverances, and wonders, all as a result of the ministry of the disciples who were filled with the Spirit in Acts 2.

In 1 Corinthians 12, Paul, a Spirit-filled leader, is writing to a Spirit-filled church teaching them about the gifts of the Spirit. This means that all of the gifts of the Spirit—wisdom, knowledge, faith, healing, miracles, prophecy, discernment of spirits, speaking in different tongues, and interpretation of tongues—were predicated on first being filled with the Spirit. This only makes sense because all of these gifts are called the 'gifts of the Spirit'. Paul says in 1 Corinthians 12:7 that these gifts are a "manifestation of the Spirit" and are "given for the common good." Only the Holy Sprit releases these gifts.

Reason 8. <u>We are commanded to desire the gifts of the Holy Spirit.</u> Paul says this in 1 Corinthians 14:1, "Follow the way of love and eagerly desire spiritual gifts." It only makes sense that if we are commanded to desire spiritual gifts then we first need to be filled with the Holy Spirit. Jesus commanded his disciples to wait until they were filled, and since we have received the same promise, this is his command to us as well. Paul says it quite definitely in Ephesians 5:18, "...be filled with the Spirit."

Luke tells us in Acts 2:39, "The promise is for you and your children and for all who are far off—for all whom the Lord our God will call." The baptism of the Spirit is a promise, and the only reason God makes a promise is because he wants us to receive it. This promise has been written several times in the Bible. In Isaiah 44:3 it says, "For I will pour water on the thirsty land, and streams on the dry ground; I will pour out my Spirit on your offspring, and my blessing on your descendants." And in Joel 2:28 it says, "And afterward, I will pour out my Spirit on all people. Your sons and daughters will prophesy, your old men will dream dreams, your young men will see visions."

Reason 9. <u>Our prayer life will be transformed.</u> Jesus said, "Out of the abundance of the heart the mouth speaks" (Matt 12:35). If our hearts are filled with the Holy Spirit, then our mouths will be filled with God's words and praise. Jesus also said that when we are filled with the Spirit, living water would flow out from within us. God wants his life and power to flow out of our lives to others. This life force of the Holy Spirit clearly empowers our prayers, giving us fresh passion, authority, and strength to fight the good fight of faith.

We see this in Acts 4:29-31. The disciples were praying and this is what is recorded: "Now, Lord, consider their threats and enable your servants to speak your word with great boldness. Stretch out your hand to heal and perform miraculous signs and wonders through the name of your holy servant Jesus." The Holy Spirit was praying through them with boldness and confidence.

In Romans, Paul gives us a little more insight into this type of prayer. Romans 8:26-27 says, "In the same way, the Spirit helps us in our weakness. We do not know what we ought to pray for, but the Spirit himself intercedes for us with groans that words cannot express. And he who searches our hearts knows the mind of the Spirit, because the Spirit intercedes for the saints in accordance with God's will." Many times we don't know how to pray. We can always rely on the Holy Spirit to help us pray according to God's will. This is why Paul writes in Ephesians 6:18, "And pray in the Spirit on all occasions." This is how we know we are praying correctly, because the Spirit is guiding our words and thoughts. Jude says the same thing in verse 20, "But you, dear friends, build yourselves up in your most holy faith and pray in the Holy Spirit."

Reason 10. <u>You will be part of a worldwide Holy Spirit phenomenon.</u> The fastest growing and largest Christian churches in the world today are all Spirit-filled. There are more Spirit-filled Christians than non-Spirit-filled Christians in the Body of Christ. In other words, you are not alone, you are not a minority, you are not part of a sect and you are not unusual. You are part of the greatest movement on planet.

There is a Christian church in Seoul, South Korea, that has over one million members. China has over 250 million Spirit-filled believers. There is a church in Argentina that has over 300,000 Spirit-filled believers, a church in Columbia with over 64,000, a church in the Ukraine of over 32,000, a church in Nigeria of over 70,000, and a church in the Ivory Coast of over 72,000. Reinhard Bonnke's ministry has reached 1.8 million people in a single meeting in Africa. Spirit-filled preachers have held the largest crusades and evangelistic meetings throughout history, all revivals, all awakenings, and Spirit-filled leaders have led all religious reformations.

What Jesus started in the book of Acts he is continuing to this day, turning the world upside down through Spirit-filled believers who minister in God's power and grace.

DEVELOPING A DEVOTIONAL LIFE

By Kenn Baird

I have always enjoyed playing rugby and Tug O' War. Both sports stretch me (sometimes literally) in my abilities and offer a challenge that helps shape character. Granted, my involvement these days is restricted to that of being an armchair expert. Nevertheless, I love these sports. Every time I watch a Tug O' War contest I remember my 'Stretch Armstrong' Christmas. 'Stretch' was an elastic-styled man who could be stretched to many times his original size, or so the statement on the toy box claimed. This particular Christmas, our youngest son had us hunting high and low for a 'Stretch Armstrong'. It was *the* toy of demand that Christmas and we joined hundreds of other parents searching for the elusive 'Stretch'. We succeeded, and on Christmas morning it was a joy to behold our son's pleasure when he opened the box. But that was to be short lived!

It was claimed that 'Stretch' was almost indestructible. Clearly the toy makers had not reckoned with 'the Baird boys'. Although that Christmas started out with joy and many happy 'Stretch Armstrong' moments occurred, the day came when our two boys engaged 'Stretch' in a Tug O' War contest just to see how far he could stretch. Would Stretch live up to the claims on the box? Was he really indestructible? Although my wife warned them repeatedly that disaster was imminent, it fell on deaf ears and the indestructible Stretch Armstrong fell apart!

Stretching requires an outside source. When you first became a follower of Jesus, what did you do? You simply said 'Yes' to God and he did the work. He changed you. God then began to work in you, to stretch you into his likeness. Read 2 Corinthians 3:18 and see what this involves.

Here is a story that shows what happens when we are over stretched. A rather incompetent best man was on the way to his best friend's wedding and he had decided to travel by air. Whilst answering a call of nature in the aircraft toilet, he decided to double-check that he still had the ring. As he held it in his hand and admired its beauty, the plane hit an air pocket and jolted. The ring fell into the toilet pan and disappeared from sight. Panicking, the best man stuck his hand into the toilet hoping to locate the lost ring, but without success.

Thinking he could perhaps see the item if he got closer, he thrust his head into the pan at which point his head became so securely stuck between the metal ridges of the integrated toilet seat that he was unable to move.

Somehow, he managed to kick the toilet door with his feet and he attracted the attention of the stewardess. She was unable to release him and so she called the pilot, who had to unscrew the top half of the metal toilet system to enable the poor man to stand up, though his head remained trapped within the square metal box.

Having taken so long for the unfortunate man's release, the plane was arriving at its destination and had begun its descent. The 'return to your seats' call was made and the embarrassed man was required to take his seat for landing. Gasps and giggles accompanied him as he walked back down the aisle with the metal toilet still on his head.

After the aircraft landed he was rushed to a service area where the airport staff took three hours to cut the man's head free from its steel entombment. The ring was also recovered, and the best man went happily on his way. He arrived late for the grand celebratory meal, which had been planned for the night before the wedding, but was relieved that his ordeal was finally over. Now it was important to make a good impression. "There will be no more embarrassing moments!" he thought.

During the meal, however, a kindly guest quietly pointed out that the best man had forgotten to do up the zipper on his trousers. The grateful man hurriedly rectified the situation, inadvertently catching his zipper in the tablecloth. At the second course, when the best man got up from the beautifully laid table with as much dignity as he could muster, he walked away carrying the table and its entire contents with him. Much of the meal landed on the lap of the bride's mother!

The man in our story went from bad to worse. God wants us to go from success to success and the key to this is developing an ever-growing daily relationship with Him. He will change us! He will stretch us!

You may fall back into the old ways of trying to change yourself, but you will only end up feeling totally frustrated. We forget that we can't change ourselves. Change only comes as we daily submit to God. He will change us, and he will stretch us. There will never be a point in your life as a follower of Jesus when God isn't stretching you. We may never be perfect until we get to heaven. But that's still our goal. We are transformed into the likeness of Jesus by the power of the Holy Spirit. Read what the Apostle Paul wrote in Philippians 3:10-14.

Here's another example of change. Alice was the chief church moaner! If moaning ever became an Olympic sport then Alice was a serious medal contender. She would moan about the weather, about the chair she sat on, about the volume of music, the length of the sermon, or the colour of the Pastor's shirt. She just liked to moan! One day someone mentioned to her that she was wasting her energy on moaning when it could be put to better use on bettering her situation. This man told her that because she was continually upset she was effectively causing herself more harm than her situation warranted. The answer did not rest on Alice being able to control her situation but rather on her controlling how she felt about it. The answer lay in a change of attitude. Alice stopped moaning and quickly people began to comment on her new attitude. Soon she was being invited to participate and shortly afterwards she became a key member of various teams within the Church. Someone once said that, "If you keep saying things are going to be bad, you have a chance of becoming a prophet!" Now read Proverbs 6:2.

We all need to be changed and this must be on a daily basis. Lasting change in the Christian life comes from spending consistent time with God. Developing a devotional time with the Lord is vital.

It's easy to have a very shallow relationship with someone. A friend of mine once told me that someone had accused him of being 'a mile wide and an inch deep'. Fellowship is what deepens a relationship. You can't have instant fellowship. If you want to really get to know somebody, you've got to spend time with him or her. To really get to know God, you need to spend time with him and ask him to teach you about himself. It begins with a sincere heart.

The secret to any ministry that I may have is really quite simple. It starts and ends with my relationship with the Lord. Often I will wait until the house is quiet, then take my Bible and sit in my favourite chair and just spend time in his presence. Busyness is the curse of this generation. Far too many would-be followers of Jesus are finding their time squeezed out by busyness. You must deal decisively with this issue if you are to develop a relationship with God. Susanna Wesley, the mother of the great evangelist and hymn writers, John and Charles Wesley, had nineteen children! There were no schools close to their home so she 'home educated' her family. She made all their clothing, cooked their meals and tended to their needs, but at one o'clock every day she retired to her room, closed the door and spent an hour just meeting with the Lord. Her children knew not to disturb her during this time. That was her secret - time spent alone with God.

Think about that for a moment. Susanna had no labour-saving devices, no washing machine, dishwasher, gas cooker, microwave, refrigerator or a deep freezer, yet she prioritised her time with God. Susanna Wesley was in effect a full-time mother, carer, teacher, wife, cook, cleaner, clothes maker and a number of other roles thrown in too. Now that's busy! But above all of this she was a woman who prioritised her daily time and relationship with God.

I love my wife and my wife loves me. We both know it and we are very secure in our marriage. The secret is that we have developed a deep and strong friendship that sits at the core of our relationship. From the day we met right up to the present, we have prioritised time to talk together and get to know each other. So it must be with your relationship with God. You must spend time developing it. He loves you, and as amazing as it might sound, he wants to spend time with you.

Now, I know a lot of people from all over the world. I have met the Queen and the Royal family several times, served as a bodyguard for the former Queen Mother, entertained senior Government Politicians in our home and met countless thousands of wonderful people as I travelled the world. However, even though I may have met them, I cannot claim that I know them. You see, I have never lived with any of these people; I have only met them. When you become a follower of Jesus, you meet him and the relationship begins. But unless you take time to become close, personal friends, you can never claim that you know him.

A sincere heart is a clean heart. As a follower of Jesus you have been forgiven through the sacrifice of Jesus Christ. His blood has cleansed you of all your sins, and God now sees you as pure and spotless. Through your devotional life you have the privilege of getting to know God. He already knows you and now you have the privilege of knowing him. But you must make it your life's number one ambition. You must make time with the Lord a number one priority.

There are lots of choices in life, and those choices will determine the priorities in our lives. So we must be careful or the 'busyness' and simple pleasures of life may crowd out our time with the Lord. We must make time for God. But lots of things can get in the way of the most important thing - God himself! John Bunyan said about the Bible: "This book will keep you from sin or sin will keep you from this book." Now read what the apostle Peter writes in 1 Peter 2:2.

In Luke 10:38-42 we read that Jesus and his disciples were in the home of two sisters named Martha and Mary. Martha was busily making preparations to serve the guests in their home, whilst Mary was sitting at the feet of Jesus listening to what he was saying. Martha complained to Jesus, "'Lord, don't you care that my sister has left me to do the work by myself? Tell her to help me!' And Jesus said to her, 'Martha, Martha...you are worried and upset about many things, but only one thing is needed. Mary has chosen what is better, and it will not be taken away from her.'"

Martha is a picture of the person who is overly involved. She's busy. She's doing a lot of stuff, and yet she doesn't reflect the life that is filled to overflowing with the peace of God and the life of God. Unlike Mary, she's anxiously and busily doing things for God. She's not really taking the time to sit and listen, to fellowship, to get to know the Lord.

In his Rectorial Address to the students of St Andrew's University, J M Barrie quoted the immortal letter which Captain Scott of the Antarctic wrote to him, when the chill breath of death was already on his expedition: "We are digging out in a very comfortless spot. We are in a desperate state, our feet are frozen, we have no fuel, and we are a long way from food. But it would do your heart good to be in our company and to hear our songs and our cheery conversation." The secret is this: Happiness depends not on things or on places, but always on people. If we are with the right person, nothing else matters; and if we are not with the right person, nothing can make up for that absence. The Lord is a Christians greatest of all friends. Nothing can separate the Christian from his presence and so nothing can take away his joy.

As mentioned earlier, there are a lot of things in life that can potentially get in the way of our fellowship with God. I love riding my Triumph motorcycle, but I have to be careful. It's really relaxing for me but I have to make sure that it doesn't consume too much of my time. Even our rest belongs to the Lord.

In Luke 8:4-15, Jesus introduces us to the Parable of the Sower. Here we discover that some people receive the word with great joy, and they're excited and really growing, but after a while life's worries, riches and pleasures come in and choke out the word, making it unfruitful. There are many kinds of worries in life. Spending time with God is the one thing that will effectively deal with worry. Now read Matthew 4:4 and Matthew 6:25 in your Bible. There will always be things that we can worry about. But as we make time for the Lord and his word, worry is replaced by faith, peace, and the assurance that God knows our needs even before we ask.

Here is a story to help you grasp this point. Many years ago in South Africa, a man sold his farm so that he might spend his days in search of diamonds. He was consumed with dreams of becoming wealthy. When he had finally exhausted his resources and his health, and was no closer to his fortune than the day he sold his farm, he threw himself into a river and drowned. One day, the man who had bought his farm spotted an unusual-looking stone in a creek bed. He placed it on a shelf as a conversation piece. A visitor noticed the stone and examined it closely. He then voiced his suspicion that it was actually a diamond. The discreet farmer had the stone analysed and found that it was one of the largest and finest diamonds ever discovered. Still operating with great secrecy, the farmer searched his stream, gathering similar stones. They were all diamonds. In fact, his farm was covered with diamonds just waiting to be picked up! The farm the diamond-seeker had sold turned out to be one of the richest diamond deposits in the world.

The lessons of wisdom can often be learned in the relationships and experiences we encounter every day. Ask God to reveal to you what you need to know in order to live the life he desires. Like the farmer, the resources you need are probably right in front of you.

Basically, there are two essential ingredients for spending time with God: the Word of God and Prayer. Start with the Bible, the Word of God, because the Bible reveals God. God is a living being. He's a person. The Bible is the Word of God, because it reveals who God is, it is one of the most necessary ingredients for having fellowship with God. We need to spend time reading the Word of God to learn about him. Not only do we need to read the Bible, but we also need to understand it and apply it to our lives.

Always begin your devotional time by praising and thanking God for who he is and what he has done, and for what he is doing and will do in your life. Here is a tip I have always taught new believers. Separate your devotions into two parts: Your Bible Reading and your Prayers.

Your Bible Reading

When you read the word of God you need to have a plan or you'll probably give up very quickly. As the saying goes, if you aim at nothing, you'll hit it every time. If your reading is planned and systematic, you will gain a better understanding of the context of a passage and come to learn the whole counsel of God rather than just bits and pieces. Your local Christian bookstore may have several selections of Bible reading plans to choose from. You might even find one in the front or back of your own Bible. Most reading plans take you through the entire Bible in one year. It doesn't take a lot of time each day, and if you will do it regularly, in just one year you will have read God's Word from cover to cover. Since we already know that the Bible reveals a living God, that's a great way to get to know him. All it takes is a real desire and a little bit of discipline and perseverance.

Make sure you deal with the known distractions. Turn on your telephone answering machine and switch off your mobile phone. Contrary to what most people think, you will survive without these for an hour! Make sure you plan ahead and find a place where you can be alone to read God's word and talk with the Lord. Here are a few suggestions to help you get the most out of your study of the Bible.

Your Personal Application: When you read, don't just read to finish a task or just so you can mark it off on your plan and feel good that you did it. Read for personal application. Pay attention to details. Ask yourself, "What's taking place here? What does God have to say? Is there a personal application for my life?"

Ask Questions: You're going to come to passages you don't understand. Ask, "Lord, what does this mean?" Even though I have been reading the Bible for many years, there are still things I don't understand. God wants us to ask questions, and he will answer many of those questions. Complete understanding will come when we see the Lord face to face.

Because I'm a pastor, some people assume (wrongly I must add) that I am totally mature spiritually and don't have faults or weaknesses. But I do have faults and weaknesses like everybody else. Just ask my wife and the people I work with. The truth is, I ask God a lot of questions all the time. I ask God about scriptures that I'm reading, about things that happen to me, and about the everyday things of life as well as the bigger events around me. It can be very interesting to keep a journal of these 'conversations with God' and to go back and read some of your questions to see how God has answered them. He doesn't always answer all of our questions immediately. Sometimes it takes a while before he gives us the answer. Now read in your Bible, Ephesians 1:17-18.

I often write down the questions I have for God. Sometimes when I'm driving to a pastoral visit or meeting, I find myself thinking about the Lord and meditating on a scripture I've read. God will then give me a thought or an insight. When I get a moment I will pull over and write it down. It can be very helpful to write down your thoughts, whether it's a question, or an insight, or an answer that God has given you.

When God tells you to do something, you should write that down too. I have a daily list of things to do. So when God specifically tells me something he wants me to do, I write it down and make it a priority on my list. Learn to listen for the little things God tells you as well as the big things. And if necessary - write it down!

Apply Actions: After God speaks to you, it's important to respond to him. God's intention is not only that we know his word, but also that we do his word. Now read in your Bible James 1:22-26:

"Do not merely listen to the word, and so deceive yourselves. Do what it says. Anyone who listens to the word but does not do what it says is like a man who looks at his face in a mirror and, after looking at himself, goes away and immediately forgets what he looks like. But the man who looks intently into the perfect law that gives freedom, and continues to do this, not forgetting what he has heard, but doing it -- he will be blessed in what he does."

Your Prayers

Look at your hand. It has five fingers (well four and a thumb!). Starting with the thumb, number your fingers 1-5. Now apply these five prayer guides to the appropriate finger.

1) Start with the THUMB: This reminds me to pray for those closest to me (my family and friends).

2) Next comes my INDEX FINGER (my pointing finger). This reminds me to pray for those who teach and instruct me (my Pastor, Leaders, etc.).

3) Next I arrive at my MIDDLE FINGER (my tallest finger). This reminds me to pray for those who stand tallest in society (the government and those in positions of authority, both locally and nationally).

4) Now I arrive at my RING FINGER (my weakest finger). This reminds me to pray for those who are weakest in society: The disabled and the sick, the homeless, the disadvantaged and abused, and the vulnerable and the broken hearted.

5) Finally I arrive at my SMALLEST FINGER (furthest from me). Now it's time to pray for myself and my own personal needs.

I have found over the years that the enemy will employ two basic tactics to hinder our devotional life: Tiredness and wandering thoughts.

Tiredness comes from the busyness of the day and if you cram your devotional life into your days end then guess what? That's correct - you find yourself tired, exhausted and falling asleep as you try to read your Bible and pray. The way to overcome this is to prioritise your devotions at the start of the day or in the middle of the day. It may also help to walk and pray as this keeps you focused. It takes a little self-discipline but will reap great rewards.

Wandering thoughts can be introduced to your mind at the strangest of times. There you are, praying away, and suddenly you find yourself planning your day or creating your shopping list. Ask the Holy Spirit to help you stay focused. I have always found it useful to read aloud and pray aloud. This way I am concentrating on what I am doing and it becomes much more difficult for my mind to be impacted with wandering thoughts.

Enjoy your devotional time. It's special and it's the key to a successful life with God.

THE POWER OF PRAYER

By Dan Chesney

Prayer is the art of talking to God. It is communication that begins in the heart and is spoken through the mouth. Prayer can be a plea, an expression of gratitude, a desperate cry, a question, a request, or a shout of praise. It can be expressed through a pause to listen, a conversation, an exchange of hearts, or an encounter. Prayer is a way to experience God himself. We exchange life with God when we pray. It is the place where we can be real, personal, open and vulnerable without pretence. Prayer is private communion with God. Prayer is relational.

It is important that we don't consider prayer to be a chore or spiritual duty but as an opportunity to meet with our Creator, the God of the universe. There is no greater privilege than to meet with God. That is why David said in Psalm 122:1, "I rejoiced with those who said to me, 'Let us go to the house of the Lord.'" That is where David met with God. And again in Psalm 16:11(NKJV), "In your presence is fullness of joy; at your right hand are pleasures forevermore." Prayer has always been more than simply speaking words. It is more about experiencing God through communication. The real joy in the life of faith is meeting with God and that happens when we pray.

Like all spiritual disciplines, prayer must be developed. Not only do we want to meet with God, we also want to receive answers to our prayers. This means there is a right way and a wrong way to pray. The wrong way would be our way. The right way is God's way, and he has revealed this way in his Word. The disciples grew up in Israel as good orthodox Jews who kept the law. They were taught how to pray, but when they saw the link between Jesus' prayer life and his ministry life, they wanted to know more about his prayer life. In Luke 11:1 they said, "...Lord, teach us to pray, just as John taught his disciples." This then led to what is now commonly known as the Lord's Prayer. It is a good model for us.

Starting in Matthew 6:5, Jesus taught them, "And when you pray, do not be like the hypocrites, for they love to pray standing in the synagogues and on the street corners to be seen by men. I tell you the truth, they have received their reward in full. But when you pray, go into your room close the door and pray to your Father, who is unseen. Then your Father, who sees what is done in secret, will reward you."

The first thing Jesus addresses is our heart attitude. Hypocrites pray to be seen by men, not to meet to with God. By their outward behaviour they want people to think they are spiritual. This is man's way of praying, and it's the wrong way. God's way is for us to find a private place where we can meet with God, because this keeps our hearts pure. This is God's way, praying from a pure heart, and this is the right way.

After dealing with the heart issues Jesus goes on to his second point, which is faith versus unbelief. He says in Matthew 6:7-8, "And when you pray, do not keep on babbling like pagans, for they think they will be heard because of their many words. Do not be like them, for your Father knows what you need before you ask him." People who do not have a personal relationship with Christ feel they have to keep on asking him for what they need because they don't know if God will answer them or not. Their prayers are often repetitive because they think the more they pray, the greater chance they have of their prayers being answered. Their faith in quantity, but we have our faith in quality. Our faith in answered prayer is not in OUR PRAYERS but in WHO GOD IS. That's why Jesus said, "...for your Father knows what you need before you ask him." This is the kind of God we serve, a Father who is waiting to give us what we need.

Once our hearts are right and our faith is in God and not ourselves, Jesus begins to give us an outline of what we are to pray for and how we are to pray. He starts in Matthew 6:9, saying, "This, then, is how you should pray: 'Our Father in heaven, hallowed be your name.'" Our first focus in prayer is to be toward our heavenly Father. We don't spend all our prayer time telling him what we want, what we need, or what our problems are. We recognise that he is our Father. How amazing! God is actually our Father, our relation, and our family. We always need to know who we're coming to, acknowledging who he is.

We also need to reverence his name. To hallow means to bless and to exalt. Let this reality set into your mind: God is your Father. Then think what a father means to you, what the role of a father is in your life, perhaps not what your earthly father was like, but what a true father is supposed to be like. God is all of that and more. He is a faithful and loving Father and he never fails.

Jesus goes on to say in Matthew 6:10, "your kingdom come, your will be done on earth as it is in heaven." Now we are praying for God's will to be done and not our own, because when we pray for God's will we always receive the answer. 1 John 5:14-15 says, "This is the confidence we have in approaching God: that if we ask anything according to his will, he hears us. And if we know that he hears us— whatever we ask—we know that we have what we asked of him." What a promise! We know that our prayers are answered. It is amazing that God would teach us to pray so that heaven would come down to earth. Who doesn't want that? Heaven is perfect, heaven is everything everybody wants or only dreams of, and we are to supposed to pray, "your kingdom come, your will be done on earth **as it is in heaven**." This means we have to know what God's will is.

How do we discover that? We do so by reading, studying and mediating on his Word, by praying and listening to his Spirit, by learning from others who are more experienced than us and have a successful prayer life, and by seeking him first in all things. The more the disciples were around Jesus, the more they understood him and trusted him, and the same will be true for us. It always comes back to relationship.

The third lesson Jesus taught is us in Matthew 6:11, "Give us today our daily bread." After worshipping the Father, after praying for God's will to be done, we can now change the focus to our own needs. It is not wrong to pray for what we need. God simply wants our hearts and priorities to be right. When we put God first, he builds our faith, strengthens our lives, and ministers to us. Now we are in a better place to receive from him. We trust him more. We come to a place where we know he loves us, so when we ask for our needs to be met, we have confidence that he will meet them.

Jesus said in Matthew 7:7-11, "Ask and it will be given to you; seek and you will find; knock and the door will be opened to you. For everyone who asks receives; he who seeks finds; and to him who knocks, the door will be opened. Which of you, if his son asks for bread, will give him a stone? Or if he asks for a fish, will give him a snake? If you, then, though you are evil, know how to give good gifts to your children, how much more will your Father in heaven give good gifts to those who ask him!" This is a solid promise of God's goodness and love toward us. He wants to give us what we need. He has already promised it before we even ask. No wonder the writer of Hebrews says in chapter 4:16, "Let us then approach the throne of grace with confidence, so that we may receive mercy and find grace to help us in our time of need." God wants us to come to him. He is our Father and he loves us.

Now we come to the fourth facet of prayer and it could prove to be one of the most difficult. Jesus teaches us to forgive. He says in Matthew 6:12, "Forgive us our debts, as we also have forgiven our debtors." The problem is not so much asking our heavenly Father to forgive us for what we have done wrong, but asking him to forgive others that have wronged, hurt, abused, misused, insulted, harmed, rejected, or abandoned us. Whatever the reason, when an injustice has been done to us, it hurts. The wounds can go deep and forgiving may not be easy.

Yet notice how this sentence is phrased, "Forgive us our debts, as we also have forgiven our debtors." Our forgiveness is contingent upon our willingness to forgive those who have hurt us. In verse 15, Jesus says, "But if you do not forgive men their sins, your Father will not forgive your sins."

This is the divine principle. Jesus forgave us first before we asked him to forgive us. Jesus did not wait for us to admit we were wrong; he absorbed our sin by looking like the one who was wrong. He looked like the criminal on the cross. This takes humility, and this is the right way to pray. Our way would be to make them suffer for what they did, but God's way is to suffer for them and extend mercy.

We are acting like Jesus when we forgive our offenders. If we will obey the Father, he will reward us, just as he did Jesus. Christ was raised in resurrection power and seated in heavenly places. We in turn will also experience his power, his pleasure, his joy, his grace; and it will far outshine the sorrow we had. Mercy triumphs over justice, love conquerors hate, good wins over evil. Romans 12:21 says, "Do not be overcome by evil, but overcome evil with good." This is exactly how you do it: forgive others first and then you too will be forgiven.

Now we begin to move into the victory Jesus describes in Matthew 6:13, "And lead us not into temptation, but deliver us from the evil one." Every Christian is tempted; every Christian is harassed by the Devil. That is why Paul says in Ephesians 6:10-13, 18, "Finally, be strong in the Lord and in his mighty power. Put on the full armor of God so that you can take your stand against the Devil's schemes. For our struggle is not against flesh and blood, but against the rulers, against the authorities, against the powers of this dark world and against the spiritual forces of evil in the heavenly realms. Therefore put on the full armor of God, so that when the day of evil comes, you may be able to stand your ground, and after you have done everything, to stand...And pray in the Spirit on all occasions with all kinds of prayers and requests. With this in mind, be alert and always keep on praying for all the saints."

Prayer and spiritual warfare go hand-in-hand. God wants us to look to him for help in this battle over darkness. He does not expect us to fight it alone. King David is a good example of this because he fought many battles, yet after hundreds of wars, he was never wounded once. Why? God was his shield, his fortress, his high tower, his protector, and his keeper. Psalm 3:3-4 says, "But you are a shield around me, O LORD...To the LORD I cry aloud, and he answers me from his holy hill." Psalm 18:3 says, "I call to the LORD, who is worthy of praise, and I am saved from my enemies." Psalm 18:29 and 33 say, "With your help I can advance against a troop; with my God I can scale a wall...He makes my feet like the feet of a deer; he enables me to stand on the heights." Psalm 23:4 says, "Even though I walk through the valley of the shadow of death, I will fear no evil, for you are with me; your rod and your staff, they comfort me."

Take all your challenges, concerns, fears, problems, hassles, worries, battles, and troubles to the Lord. He wants to help you. He knows how to deliver us from evil.

And finally, the Christ's prayer ends with an awesome crescendo of praise as Jesus tells his disciples in Matthew 6:13 (NKJV) "For yours is the kingdom and the power and the glory forever, Amen." This is the way to end your prayers - with praise, adoration, a shout of victory, and an acknowledgement of God's great power over everything that would attempt to defeat you. It is only right that we give him all the praise, every honour, all the accolades, and all the thanks him for who he is and what he has done for us.

The book of Psalms is our hymnbook. It teaches us how to praise our Father. As you start coming to the end of the book, it grows in praise to our God, until it ends with a call for universal worship from nature, mankind, and all of heaven. Praise is our declaration of faith in God; it is the voice of gratitude, of appreciation, of our love for him. As Paul says in 1 Thessalonians 5:16-18, "Be joyful always; pray continually; give thanks in all circumstances, for this is God's will for you in Christ Jesus." And again in Philippians 4:4, "Rejoice in the Lord always. I will say it again: Rejoice!" And in Colossians 3:17, "And whatever you do, whether in word or deed, do it all in the name of the Lord Jesus, giving thanks to God the Father through him." This is to be a lifelong habit, being thankful at all times in all situations, because we know we serve a God who answers prayer.

Jesus gave this prayer as a starting point for us. It is a simple model. But it is not the only prayer he wants us to pray. As our relationship grows, so will our prayer life. When you read through the Psalms you will discover that they are actually prayers, and there are 150 of them. There are also many other prayers in the Bible that were offered up by men and women in all kinds of situations. They are examples left for us to learn from, but the greatest prayer we can ever pray is one that comes from our own heart. It is one thing for a mother to tell her husband that their children love him, but it is another thing for the father to hear it himself from his own children. And it is the same for us. God wants to hear from us, from our heart, because that is real. In the end, God wants us to be real with him.

So pray using your own words, pray in your own style, whether on your knees, standing, with your eyes closed or open, lying on your bed or sitting in a chair, out in a field, walking through a park, in your car, on a bike, floating on a lake, or in your closet. Remember, God looks at the heart because that is the real us.

As David said in Psalm 19:14, "May the words of my mouth and the meditation of my heart be pleasing in your sight, O LORD, my Rock and my Redeemer." When we pray from the heart God hears that more than our words.

COMMUNION

By Kenn Baird

Now that are a Christian I thought it appropriate to introduce you to the topic of Communion.

Communion, the Breaking of Bread, the Lord's Table, Agape Feast, the Eucharist....you will hear many names given to this act of remembrance in different churches.

On the night when the people of Israel were brought out of slavery in Egypt, a lamb was killed, roasted and eaten. Its blood was smeared on the doorposts of their houses, marking them so the Angel of death would 'passed over'. This was the source of the Jewish feast of Passover. You can read about this in Exodus 12.

The night before he was betrayed and crucified, Jesus celebrated the Passover Feast with his disciples. The Bible calls this event the 'Last Supper'. You can read about it in Matthew 26:17-30, Mark 14:12-26, Luke 22:1-23, 1 Corinthians 11:23-25. During the meal, Jesus instructed his followers to 'remember' him. You can read this in Luke 22:1-23.

"And he took bread, gave thanks and broke it, and gave it to them saying, 'This is my body given for you; do this in remembrance of me.' In the same way, after the supper he took the cup, saying, 'This cup is the new covenant in my blood, which is poured out for you,'" (Luke 22:20-21).

There are two symbolic elements used in our remembrance ceremony which we now call the Communion Service: the bread (representing Jesus body) and the wine (representing his blood). The bread reminds us that Jesus' body was broken for us and that he took in his body the punishment for our sins. Read Isaiah 53. Note carefully the phrase in verse 5, "...by his wounds we are healed." The cup of wine represents Christ's blood and reminds us that we have forgiveness through the shed blood of Jesus.

All of us are unworthy to have communion with Jesus but through His atoning work, we are made worthy and afforded this great privilege. It is the manner of our taking and our attitude towards others that can render us unworthy.

The Apostle Paul rebuked the Corinthian Church regarding their attitude (1 Corinthians 11). The Corinthians did not properly discern or recognise the Lord's Table. The wealthy were shaming the poor through selfish eating practices (verse 21-22) and in doing so, were not discerning the true nature of the church as Christ's body in which all social and racial differences are blotted out (Galatians 3:28).

So we can see that Communion is a covenant act of remembrance (Luke 22:19) by which we express our thanks to God for the sacrifice of his Son. It is also a time for proclaiming the Lord's death (1 Corinthians 11:26) and participating in what Jesus has done for us on the Cross.

We can translate this into three fundamental truths. It is a time of remembrance, thanksgiving and expressing our deepest praise and appreciation for all Jesus has done for us, and a memorial to his death and finished work. It is a time for refreshing through participating in the benefits of Jesus' death and resurrection. In doing so we receive refreshment from Jesus through the Holy Spirit. (Read about this in Romans 5:10, and 1 Corinthians 10:16). And it is a time for recommitment (1Corinthians 11:28-29), a statement of the return of Christ and a statement of 'One Body' - his Church.

The Bible does not prescribe a religious formula for Communion. We are told that it is 'whenever' (1 Corinthians 11:25-26) and not how many times or on what occasions or in which locations. You might like to look at Acts 2:46 and see how the early church celebrated Communion in homes and at meal times. The Bible makes no mention of a clergyman being the only one who can serve Communion. You might like to do this in your home with friends as part of a meal or during a time of worship.

What is important is that you remember the great importance prescribed in the Scripture: "For whenever you eat this bread and drink this cup, you proclaim the Lord's death until he comes" (1 Corinthians 11:26).

TITHES AND OFFERINGS

By Kenn Baird

I'm glad that you have taken a moment to read through this booklet and I pray that the Holy Spirit will open up the scriptures to you as you read. In the next few pages you will learn how to biblically handle money and move into the blessing of obedience to your heavenly Father.

In Acts 20:27-31 we read how the Apostle Paul did not hold back from speaking the whole council of God. Holding back from teaching what God has to say about finances (or indeed any subject) is to fail to declare his revelation on the subject. Satan is a liar, and he would have you enter into a guilt trip with regard to this subject. He questions motives and sows suspicion of leadership. Our materialistic, self-serving generation is wide open to his manipulation, especially when it comes to money. Basically, the truth is simply this: Many Christians just don't trust God to provide for them and instead have their lives led by a 'self–first' motivation.

Jesus clearly states that you cannot serve God and money (Matthew 6:24). This is a principle for life; God must always come first. Our society declares the opposite and people end up living for money. Your very identity can be influenced by it, governments have been corrupted by it, and people have starved through a lack of it.

Here are a couple of biblical warnings concerning money to consider:

1) Psalm 62:10 - Do not set your heart on riches.

2) 1 Timothy 6:9-10 - Love of money is the root of all kinds of evil.

Money itself is not the problem. After all, it is just pieces of metal and paper to which we attribute worth at various levels. It's the love of money, the need for it and the worship of it that becomes the problem. People assign morality to money. Put simply, money can be a blessing or a curse depending on your attitude and approach to it.

Billy Graham once said, "If a man gets his attitude towards money straight, it will help straighten out almost every other area of his life." God must always be the source of all in our lives or else he is the solution to nothing. God's principles for our success in all areas of life is that we seek first his Kingdom and then, other things will be added to our lives (Matthew 6:33).

We must ask ourselves this question: Do we give our finances to men or to God? Remember, our giving should be motivated by a desire to see God's Kingdom extended without any expectation of personal reward except the joy of seeing souls saved and the Church multiplied.

Let's examine Matthew 23:23-24. Here we find that the religious people of the day had come to regard the letter of the law more than its spirit. They gave their tithes but not themselves. They strained minute legal 'gnats' but swallowed whole 'camels' of pride, scorn, avarice and falsehood. Jesus never criticised them for tithing. He faulted their failure to show faith, justice and mercy, with their money. In fact, Jesus says we ought to tithe. This is a moral imperative. Tithing is not a legalistic practice belonging to the Old Testament.

Consider the following verses carefully.

Hebrews 7:1-3, 5-9 tells us that Abraham tithed long before the law was written (Genesis 14:17-20). Tithing precedes the law and pertains to a higher order of Priesthood, which Jesus fulfils.

In Genesis 28:22 we find that Jacob tithed. Tithing remains God's financial plan for material support of the church and the Gospel.

The Law of Moses prescribed tithing in detailed ways that were different from Abraham and Jacob's tithe. Read Leviticus 27:30-32.

Prosperity is the result of a righteous life (Psalm 1:1-3). This applies to every area of our lives including money. Please understand me clearly at this point. I am not advocating a 'prosperity teaching' that claims that God wants you rich. I am, however, saying that we must learn to apply and live by biblical truths. God deals with us in terms of our needs and not our wants.

Poverty is an enemy of mankind, but there is a huge difference between being poor and living in poverty. A 'poverty mindset' affects both the rich and the poor alike. It is a crippling fear of never having enough that can crowd out God's call to seek first his Kingdom. In short, a poverty mindset is a fear of not being in control of your life and your future.

In Malachi 3:8-10, we read that God promises to "rebuke the devourer." Jesus also informs us that the "thief comes to steal and destroy" (John 10:10). This applies to our finances as well as every other area of life. Through learning to let go of a poverty mindset, we enter into the reality of God's promises to deal with the forces that seek to devour our finances.

Tithing is essential. God's promise of provision and protection is for those who tithe. God's promise encompasses every area of life and not just finances, but it does include finances! Tithing is the visible, open evidence that you place your dependency on God and not upon material wealth. Jesus commended the widow in the story found in Matthew 12:44 for giving out of her need and not of her plenty.

Agreement is basic to life. Read Amos 3:3. "Do two walk together unless they have agreed to do so?" Here we find another Kingdom principle that applies to every area of life, including finances. Are you in agreement with God? He wants you to trust him with your finances. God does not need your money. He simply wants you to totally depend upon him and not your money.

We live in an easy credit society. Every time I enter a store I am confronted by a sales assistant offering me some form of instant credit usually in the shape of a store charge card with its hidden interest rates. Spend now pay later is the mantra preached loudly in 21st Century Britain. But God does not want his children to live in debt. Debt blinds us to life's priorities. It is very hard to seek first the Kingdom of God when you are living in worry over your indebtedness. Your life is worth so much more than that. You were born debt free. Make it your aim to live that way.

Read Romans 13:8 and make a list of ways you can put this into action. Cancel those store cards and credit cards and look to the Lord for your provision. It is not your financial status that connects you to God's love. It is your faith. If you are reading this and find yourself in debt then let me encourage you to deal with the negative by taking a positive action. Communicate your situation with those to whom you are indebted. Make it a pressing goal to speak with your Pastor and leaders and seek their spiritual support. They will be able to guide you to people who are specialized to help with your situation. And they can pray for you as you take steps to build godly character into your life in this important area.

Windows of Blessing

God's ability to renew his purpose in our lives is dependent on our acceptance of Jesus as our Lord and Saviour. Through this act, the salvation covenant is established and God will fulfil his purpose in us as long as we are obedient to the principles of his word. At the point you receive Jesus as Lord and Saviour, you are saved for eternity, but you must also learn to allow more of God's grace and purpose to flow into your life in the 'here and now'.

The Bible talks about God being robbed and at first this might seem strange. It simply means that God has been robbed of the opportunity to bless you. Incredible! He loves you so much that he constantly wants to bless you and it grieves the heart of God when our disobedience prevents his blessing from flowing into your lives. When there is no blessing, cursing floods in and that is a real problem. When we depart from God's ways or neglect his principles, his intended blessing turns inside out. Our disobedience inverts his word. It becomes the opposite of blessing, not because God changed but because we turned away from following his ways.

In Malachi 3:7, God cries, "Return to me." Our Father God is a God of blessing and not of destruction. It is certainly true that God makes no legal demand linking tithing to salvation. However, there is a principle here that God has wrapped into the very structure of Creation. As we learn to let go of our money, give and release it as God directs, room is made in our lives for the abundance of Christ's life to flow into our life.

Why Should We Tithe?

We should tithe for four simple reasons:

1) To follow a biblical precedent.

2) To financially support the church in its ministry.

3) As an act of worship with our material substance.

4) To financially support our Pastors and Teachers (Galatians 6:6).

Where Should We Tithe?

Tithes are always given to the local Church we attend, our spiritual home. There are a great many good causes in the Christian world but our support of these should be of the nature of 'Free Will Offerings'.

When Should We Tithe?

Your tithe should be given as often as you receive salary or payment. Paul recommended that tithes should be given to your local church on the first day of the week (1 Cor. 16:2). Tithing is not an occasional gift; it is a regular habit. Tithing is the basis of a believer's giving but not the full extent of it. Through tithing we support the local church and in doing so support ourselves because the local church family is our primary source of life support.

A Word About Free Will Offerings

'Free Will Offering' is the biblical expression for giving over and above our tithes. We may perhaps give to Missions or other Christian organisations or support individuals in their ministry. Free Will giving is a giving that has no personal benefit to us. Therefore it is an act of generosity and a mark of special grace. Through tithing we share in the upkeep of the church and its ministries but through our Free Will Offerings, over and above the tithe, we show ourselves to be rich in the grace of God and filled with the love of Christ.

One of the most tragic stories I have encountered in the New Testament is the story of the *Rich Young Ruler* (Matthew 19:16-22). Here we read of a young man who backed away from discipleship because Jesus would have assumed Lordship over his finances.

The man's problem was not his money but rather his mindset. His possessions possessed him! You must develop a willingness to change in your thinking and in your attitude in order to grow into the full stature God has for you. You must learn not only to ask but also to answer the hard questions of the Christian life. Is Christ really Lord of your life? Matthew 6:21 shows how proof of his Lordship lies in the way you handle your life -- including your money. Riches are not the problem. There were many rich people following Jesus: Joseph of Arimathea, Nicodemus, Zacchaeus, etc. No, the problem is not being rich but being attached to our money in a wrong way. This kind of attitude must change! And only God can change a man's heart. Therefore, seek first his Kingdom.

Now that you have explored the subject of tithing, it's time to put what you have learned into practise. Ask the Lord to help you change your mindset and let go of any poverty thinking you may have. Ask him to fill you afresh with his Holy Spirit and release you in your finances. Having done that, reorder your spending and budget your income to give the first tenth to the Lord, affording him the opportunity to rebuke the devourer from your life.

Enjoy your new-found liberty in the Lord and rejoice that you are now participating in the Kingdom of God, helping to spread the Gospel through the giving of your tithes.

DEVELOPING A LIFESTYLE OF GIVING

By Dan Chesney

Giving is a natural part of life and we can see this in relationships - parents love their children, grandparents spoil their grandkids, friends treat their friends with gifts for birthdays, anniversaries, weddings and special occasions, employers give Christmas parties, cities throw parades with food for the public, and governments set national holidays. Giving is a part of our culture, our families and our lives on many levels. But God calls us to a different kind of giving. God calls us to generosity.

Giving is a part of God's relationship with the world. We can see this in his character. John 3:16 says, "For God so loved the world that he gave his one and only Son". It's God's nature to love and to give, and now that we have been given his life and nature, this generous spirit has become our nature too.

Giving is the fruit of love and as 1 John 4:7 says, "Dear friends, let us love one another, for love comes from God. Everyone who loves has been born of God and knows God. Whoever does not love does not know God, because God is love." This is not the kind of giving we are use. God's love is never selfish. It's sacrificial, generous, unrelenting, exuberant, abundant and without measure. God gives his all - not just what we need, but more than enough.

God's generous nature can be seen in the promises he makes to us. John 15:7 say, "If you remain in me, and my words remain in you, ask

whatever you wish and it will be given you." God is certainly not holding anything back from us in this promise. 2 Corinthians 9:8, "And God is able to make **all** grace abound to you, so that in **all** things at **all** times, having **all** that you need, you will **abound** in every good work." God's love extends unlimited giving to us. Ephesians 1:3, "Praise be to the God and Father of our Lord Jesus Christ, who has **blessed** us in the heavenly realms with **every** spiritual blessing in Christ." Our heavenly father gives according to his nature, not according to what we deserve, but according to who he is, and he is good, full of grace, mercy, kindness, and love. Ephesians 3:20, "Now to him who is able to do **immeasurably more** than all we **ask or imagine**, according to his power that is at work within us". This is a *WOW* verse because it's telling us our imagination is too small to comprehend all that God can give us. 2 Peter 1:3, "His divine power has given us **everything** we need for life and godliness through our knowledge of him who called us by his own glory and goodness." God is all- powerful and he can use his power in any way he chooses. His choice is to bless us.

Does this sound like a small-minded God? These are the words of a big-hearted God who loves to be generous! And he applies this principle of generosity to us. In Luke 6:38 Jesus tells us, "Give, and it will be given to you. A good measure, pressed down, shaken together and running over, will be poured into your lap." Here we see that when we begin to live God's lifestyle of generosity, the outcome is far greater than the measure of our giving.

Page after page of the Bible reveals God's generous spirit, and since we are his children, he wants us to be like him. We carry his DNA, we reflect his glory, and we bear his name. Jesus said this to us in Matthew 5:48, "Be perfect, therefore, as your heavenly Father is perfect." Becoming a generous person is our destiny, our nature and our calling.

One of Christ's disciples was John. He was very close to Jesus and it was referred to as the disciple that Christ loved, or John the Beloved. In 1 John 3:16-17 John connected the love of God with generosity toward others who have less than us: "This is how we know what love is; Jesus Christ laid down his life for us. And we ought to lay down our lives for our brothers. If anyone has material possessions and sees his brother in need but has no pity on him, how can the love of God be in him?" In other words, if we truly do have the love of God in our hearts, then it will produce the same spirit of compassion that leads to helping and giving to others.

God's nature of love is best seen in the work of Jesus Christ on the cross when he laid down his life to save us. On the cross Jesus made a way for us to be free from sin, sickness, fear, anxiety and poverty. 2 Corinthians 8:9, "For you know the grace of our Lord Jesus Christ, that though he was rich, yet for your sakes he became poor, so that you through his poverty might become rich." Christ gave away all of the riches of heaven for our blessing.

And this is the great principle that governs all of life, the law of giving and receiving, sowing and reaping. The world teaches us to get what we can for ourselves and then give a portion of what we have to others. God says we must give first, even from the little we have, and then he will make sure we receive what we need.

In the natural realm this is easy to see. Before a farmer can produce a crop he has to sow his seed. Before a businessman can succeed, his money must be invested. Before a person can have friends, they must be friendly. And before payday, there is a time of work. In the spiritual realm Jesus establishes this same law. In John 12:24 he says, "I tell you the truth, unless a kernel of wheat falls to the ground and dies, it remains only a single seed. But if it dies, it produces many seeds. The man who loves his life will lose it, while the man who hates his life in this world will keep it for eternal life." Jesus was referring to his death on the cross. He was the kernel of wheat that fell into the grave. By dying Jesus was going to bring many sons to glory. We are those sons; we are the fruit, the harvest of the cross. Now we, like him, must be willing to lay our life down so many others can be won for Christ. There can be no harvest of souls without giving.

This principle of giving and receiving in the spiritual and natural realm also applies to money. It's how God blesses us. Proverbs, which is the business manual in the Bible written by the wealthiest person in all of history, tells us in chapter 3:9-10, "Honour the Lord with your wealth, with the first fruits of all your crops; then your barns will be filled to overflowing, and your vats will brim over with new wine." Even though Solomon is using farmers and winemakers as examples, he is laying out a principle for people every occupation. We give a portion of our income to the Lord, and He takes that gift and multiplies it back to us. It's the miracle of increase.

The Israelites experienced many hardships so God sent Malachi the prophet to help them. He explained that one of the reasons they were suffering was that they had stopped being generous. "Ever since the time of our forefathers you have turned away from my decrees and have not kept them. 'Return to me, and I will return to you,' says the Lord Almighty. But you ask, 'How are we to return?' Will a man rob God? Yet you rob me. But you ask, 'How do we rob you?' In tithes and offerings. You are under a curse – the whole nation of you – because you are robbing me. Bring the whole tithe into the storehouse, that there may be food in my house. Test me in this,' says the Lord Almighty, 'and see if I will not throw open the floodgates of heaven and pour out so much blessing that you will not have room enough for it. I will prevent pests from devouring your crops, and the vines in your fields will not cast their fruit,' says the Lord Almighty. 'Then all nations will call you blessed, for yours will be a delightful land,'" Malachi 3:6-12.

God was making several points here. First, he was linking income with this principle of giving a portion to God. (This is called tithing and we covered this important topic in more detail in the previous chapter.) Secondly, we learn that their attitude was important. Thirdly, they were harming themselves by not giving. And fourthly, if they would repent and return to God out of an obedient heart, the measure that God would pour out on them would be more than they could manage. Now that is a generous God. Imagine having more money than you could manage because you gave to God out of a generous heart! This was his promise to Israel, and it's still his promise to us.

The Apostle Paul tells us why we are harmed by not being generous with our giving to the Lord in 2 Corinthians 9:10. "Now he who supplies seed to the sower and bread for food will also supply and increase your store of seed and will enlarge the harvest of your righteousness." This is an important scripture because it gives us several principles to managing our finances. First, it's God who gives us both the seed and the bread. The seed and the bread refer to the money we receive from our salary, our wage packet, or from any other source. If you were to receive £250 for your weekly pay, some of that is seed and some of that is bread. The seed according to this verse is for sowing, for giving to the Lord. The bread is for eating, for paying your bills and sustaining your life.

If we were to sow all of the money we receive then we would not have any bread to eat, and if we were to eat all of it as bread, than we would have nothing to sow. We have to discover from the Lord how much of our income is for sowing and how much is for bread or for meeting our needs. This is how we make Jesus Lord of our finances. This is how we become good stewards of our resources. And this is how we develop a lifestyle of giving. God may want us to sow all of our income at certain moments, but that would be unusual. For the most part, he wants us to give him a portion because it is also his will that our needs be met. If you sow all of the money you have and God meant for some of it to be your bread, the portion you sowed that was bread will not produce a harvest. When you put bread into the ground it will simply become mouldy. It cannot reproduce. Seed is for sowing and bread is for eating.

Conversely, if we eat all of our weekly pay, use it all for managing our needs, then what was meant for sowing will not be sown. This means there will be no harvest awaiting us in the future. And this is how we hurt ourselves; we can put ourselves into famine and lack because we are not sowing for future harvest. This is what the Israelites did - they consumed everything for themselves and ended up in famine. They didn't trust the Lord to take care of them. They trusted in themselves to administer their own affairs.

What is so amazing about this lesson is that God will not only bless our harvest when we sow but he will also increase our seed. Any farmer knows that the more seed you sow the greater the harvest. Paul even wrote about this in 2 Corinthians 9:6-7, "Remember this: Whoever sows sparingly will also reap sparingly, and whoever sows generously will also reap generously. Each man should give what he has decided in his heart to give, not reluctantly or under compulsion, for God loves a cheerful giver." God is actually saying that we have a part in determining our harvest, our income and our financial situation. The Israelites gave nothing and so became impoverished. But we don't have to be like that. We can learn to give generously and reap generously. We can develop a lifestyle of giving.

God does not want us to give because we have too, but because we want to, because we love to. This brings joy to our heavenly Father. Giving to God will always bring blessings. We have two extraordinary stories in Acts that highlight this. One is in chapter nine. A woman named Dorcas became sick and died very suddenly. It took the whole church by surprise. What is striking about this incident is that the local church did not call the police, or the hospital, or the undertakers, or the relatives to make arrangements for the funeral. No, they called for a man of God to come and pray. They wanted this woman to be raised from the dead! They loved her. And she was of great value to this church because she was a generous giver.

When Peter came to pray for her to be raised from the dead, it says the people showed, "him the robes and other clothing that Dorcas had made while she was still with them", that she "was always doing good and helping the poor". Her generous, giving heart generated faith in the congregation that led to her miracle of being raised from the dead.

The second story is in chapter 10. A military leader named Cornelius was seeking the true God. God heard his prayers and again sent Peter to go to his house and lead his whole family to Christ. Like Dorcas, this was a miracle because Cornelius was the first Gentile or non-Jewish believer to become a Christian. This broke down racial lines, religious lines, theological lines and historic lines. It was a monumental shift in thinking and faith. This breakthrough happened because Cornelius was a generous giver. Acts 10:2-4 say that, "He gave generously to those in need...[and his] gifts to the poor have come up as a memorial offering before God." God honours people with generous hearts. He hears their prayers. He pours out his blessings. He brings miracles into their lives. Yes, God does "love a cheerful giver."

When my wife and I were young Christians, our love for the Lord gave us a desire to want to give something back to him. We started praying about this, and what we felt he was saying to us was to give him ten percent of our income. We were overjoyed. Not only had he heard our prayers, but also he had answered us. The following year we prayed again and this time we believed he was leading us to give 17 percent. This was an exciting adventure for us as we were experiencing first-hand the joy of giving and receiving. We prayed again the third year and the word of the Lord for us was 27 percent. It was wonderful to hear God so precisely, but now this was going to require faith on our part to believe him for the bread to meet all our needs. That year we saw God supply in unexpected ways. It kept us on our knees but it was thrilling to see God move in our lives. The following year we prayed again, and this year it was, yes, 37 percent. With joy we gave, and again we saw more miracles of provision. This grew our faith and trust in God as our faithful Father and Provider.

The next year God said that we would be giving our lives. We did not know what that meant until he called us to be missionaries in England. We left our family, friend, and home in the United States with no support, no ministry, just faith in God that he was our Provider and he had never failed us. That was 26 years ago and he has provided faithfully. We have travelled thousands of miles around the world, moved houses 29 times, raised three children and never once have we not been able to pay a bill. God has not only met our needs but has done abundantly more than we could ever imagine. We have had an adventure of a lifetime, and it all started by sowing a little seed. Just like those verses said, he increased our seed year after year so we could increase our sowing, and the harvest has never stopped growing.

If you want a harvest, than learn to sow in faith. And keep on sowing because you will also need a harvest. The principal is simple. As David said in Psalms 40:4, "blessed is the man who makes the Lord his trust". Develop a lifestyle of giving.

Becoming a Witness

By Nori Chesney

DOING SOMETHING GREAT

Welcome to the Family! Making the decision to accept Jesus Christ as your personal Saviour is the most important event of your life. You will never be the same, your future is transformed, and your eternal destination is Heaven itself. This IS fantastic, amazing Good News!

Just as we feel compelled to tell someone when something good happens to us, our salvation is no different. In fact, letting others around us know about the life-changing relationship we now have with Jesus is part of God's plan for our lives, a big part, so big that the Bible refers to it as the 'Great Commission'.

It's 'great' not only because of the impact Christ has on our lives but also because the task is so big. Every individual in every generation needs to personally hear the truth about who Jesus really is so they can make an informed choice about accepting him as their Lord and Saviour. That only happens as we share the Good News with people we know and meet.

Another 'great' thing is that you don't have to wait until you've read the Bible cover-to-cover or go to a course or pass a test. In Matthew 28:19 Jesus told the Christians around him to, "Go therefore and make disciples of all the nations, baptising them in the name of the

Father and the Son and the Holy Spirit." It is a responsibility that we all share.

It is also a 'great' privilege – someone, maybe several people over many years, took the time to tell us about Christ. They did this because they care about us but also because they were following the leading of the Holy Spirit. God is the one who really cares. He makes sure that the right people come across our path at just the right moment, sharing, praying, helping us discover that Jesus is the "Way, the Truth and the Life" (John 14:1).

2 Corinthians 5:18-19 tells us, "...all of this is a gift from God, who brought us back to himself through Christ. And God has given us this task of reconciling the world to himself, no longer counting people's sins against them. And he gave us this wonderful message of reconciliation. So we are Christ's ambassadors; God is making his appeal through us. We speak for Christ when we plead, 'Come back to God!' For God made Christ, who never sinned, to be the offering for our sin, so that we could be made right with God through Christ." (NLT)

So understanding God's heart gives you a starting point to know how much he cares for the whole world. He gave you the gift of his son and now he asks you to pass on the privilege of knowing Christ.

We actually get to know God more as we share his love with others. That's why people who are brand new Christians are so good at being a witness for Jesus. Watch your relationship with God grow stronger as you experience the joy of leading a friend or family member to the Lord. It really is one of the most rewarding experiences in life. Just like it says in Philemon 6, "I am praying that you put into action the generosity that comes from your faith as you understand and experience all the good things we have in Christ."

HOW IS IT DONE?

Jesus was personally involved in people's lives. He ate, slept, prayed, traveled, and suffered with his followers; sharing his life with them daily so they could learn how to live theirs for God. What he said mattered. He was their example.

72

The first four books of the New Testament commonly referred to as the Gospels, record Christ's birth, life, death and resurrection. And just like the life of Christ, the Gospels are designed by God to teach us how to live our lives as Christians. Christ is *our* example too. His words are more than suggestions for our own personal happiness. They are divine truths spoken deliberately and recorded faithfully, and they are meant to be passed on to others.

This is **HOW** we are to witness – just like Jesus did - because he is our example. Let's look at some of the distinctive of Christ's witness.

- He always prayed first: Jesus knew how God felt about people and what God wanted to give them because he prayed daily for those around him. He had God's heart for others.

- He was inclusive: Jesus shared with anyone and everyone who cared to listen to him. He was neither prejudice nor exclusive with the Truth about who he was.

- He told stories: Using a common method of teaching called Parables, Jesus helped people understand divine concepts by using everyday examples they could relate to. His message was, 'Keep it simple'.

- He used variety: Jesus used many methods to reach as many people as possible during his brief public ministry.

- He was approachable: Jesus was warm, non-judgmental, accepting and kind to anyone with a seeking heart.

- He knew when to walk away: Jesus never pressed people who weren't ready, never forced people to accept Him if they didn't believe in Him.

- He knew what was in their hearts: Jesus understood that not everyone would accept Him as the Saviour. He always followed the promptings of the Holy Spirit when speaking to people about spiritual truth.

- He knew how to 'close the deal': Jesus always pressed through opposition to finish the task and lead people into salvation. I

73

call this closing the deal. No matter how hard it was, Jesus kept "speaking the truth in love" until the person had received full forgiveness of their sins through saving faith in him.

As you begin to share your faith with others, study these distinctives in the Gospels. Pray, seek God first, and follow his lead. He knows the people around you, knows their hearts and lives better than you ever could, and He loves them more than you ever will.

Trust the Holy Spirit to show you what to say when the opportunity presents itself to be a witness. You have Christ's word on it: "I will send you the Advocate – the Spirit of truth. He will come to you from the Father and will testify all about me" John 15:26 NLT.

Let me give you some personal examples to help illustrate how to be a witness. I grew up not knowing much about God. Through a series of personal tragedies I became angry and very mistrusting of people. This made it difficult for the few people who tried to tell me that Jesus loves me because I always rejected their attempts to be kind to me.

And they really tried! They would pray for me, out loud and in person, sometimes with tears in their eyes. They would write me notes and share Bible scriptures with me. They would invite me to join them at church services or special Christian events where they knew I would hear the Gospel. And they gave me their sincere attention, spending hours talking to me about the Lord, answering my cynical questions with patience, love and good humour. They were saints! And I was the devil's advocate.

The truth was, I was afraid and alone. Even though I argued and bullied the Christians around me who dared to speak to me, my heart was crying out to them like a little child, pleading that they would not give up on me. I was testing the love they said they had for me. And I was testing God. I didn't really believe anyone could love me or that God would forgive me of all the mistakes I had made.

Finally, after hearing the story of the Cross several times and even reading the Bible for a few weeks, I found myself all alone, walking down a mountain path. And I just started talking to God. In my heart I said these words:

"God, if you're real, and Jesus, if you are who they say you are, you can have my sorry life because it isn't worth anything to me any more."

The next thing I knew, I was walking into a tunnel of Living Light and I knew I was in the presence of a Holy God. And for the first time in a long time, I felt unashamed. All the fear and discouragement was gone. My heart was filled with peace as I realized I had actually been FORGIVEN and ACCEPTED by God. It was just like those Christians told me it would be: "For God so love the world that he gave his only begotten Son, that whoever believes in him would not perish but have everlasting life." John 3:16 NKJV

Notice some of the steps I had to go through in my journey to finding Christ.

- Christians who knew me were praying for me.

- They included me in their circle of friends even though I was very different.

- I found out how several other people had become Christians by listening to their stories.

- They used a wide variety of 'divine ideas' to try and share their faith with me, trying new approaches when I refused to respond.

- Even when I hurt them, they continued to be kind and loving toward me. They kept forgiving me even when I was hateful to them.

- When I shut down, they gave me space but they didn't abandon me. This would have proven to me that they really didn't care after all. They waited until the Holy Spirit prompted them with fresh faith and a new idea, and then they tried again.

- They believed for me! And Jesus did not disappoint them. One of the highlights of that year in school was the day I told them I had decided to give my heart to Christ.

- They knew how to close the deal. They shared the sinner's prayer with me many times before I finally said it for myself and meant it. And just as they had promised me, it worked! When the time was right and my heart was ready, I prayed a simple prayer of repentance and surrender, and Christ gave me his New Life!

I'm using my own experience as an example but you have your own story to tell now. Because God makes each person unique, there are no formulas for salvation. To be a witness, a Christian who knows the heart of God for others and who knows how to share this love, we must learn to live by the truth of Romans 1:16: "For I am not ashamed of the gospel of Christ, for it is the power of God to salvation for everyone who believes..."

WHO AND WHERE

On his very last day on earth, as he was preparing to ascend up to Heaven in plain view of his disciples, Jesus gave his final and most important word of instruction. We find it recorded in Acts 1:8, "But you will receive power when the Holy Spirit comes on you; and you will be my witnesses in Jerusalem, and in Judea and Samaria, and to the ends of the earth." This gives us insight into where we are to witness and who we are to reach.

There are four separate places listed in this verse. They represent different geographic locations but they can also describe different fields or areas where we can be a witness without leaving town.

JERUSALEM: This represents our home, our immediate circle of family and friends, those around us who know us and have regular access to our lives. We don't have to go anywhere to witness to them. We already have a relationship and regular contact. These are the people we think of first. We care about them. We want them to have what we have, and we want them to live forever with us in heaven. And so we must go to our Jerusalem, our family and friends, and tell them about Jesus.

But we must follow the wisdom of the Holy Spirit. He knows who is ready and who is not. Remember, Jesus promised that the Holy Spirit would help us, comfort us, and lead us into all the truth? Jesus never did or said anything that he didn't hear the Father tell him. And look at all the trouble that caused him!

Being a witness is not always popular, especially in a world filled with so much tension and strife over religion. Jesus himself was rejected by his Jerusalem. His own family and friends didn't believe in him until after the Resurrection. The important point is to pray for them, obey the leading of the Holy Spirit as you seek to share your faith with them, and forgive them if they reject you. Never give up on your Jerusalem!

JUDEA: These are people outside of your immediate circle of acquaintances who live in your general area. They are the people in the shops, on the high street, at school and work, people you don't know personally but come into contact with regularly. This is your Judea. These people are part of your field of harvest because they live all around you.

It may seem harder to reach them because you don't know them personally. But this is where your heart attitude can make all the difference. Jesus said, "You should love your neighbor as yourself." Matthew 22:39 He called this the second great commandment. Loving your neighbor means to care about their eternity. The people who walk past you on the street of your town, who stand in the queue at the shops, and who work alongside you, all have an uncertain eternity without Christ.

Our hearts compel us to be a witness with our actions so that, when the time comes for us to speak to them about Christ, we have laid a good foundation. It is never easy. We have to face our fears and step out in obedience each time we witness, especially to strangers. But through faith and patience we can be effective.

Don't let the culture stop you. Don't let negative attitudes stop you. Don't let fear of the unknown stop you. Don't let anything stop you from sharing the love of God with the people around you. Through the love of God and the power of the Holy Spirit, your witness to your Judea will lead people to Christ.

SAMARIA: This is what I call 'the scary people', people who are not at all like us, who don't seem to have anything in common with us, and who may actually be hostile toward Christianity. In the Bible, Jews and Samaritans were enemies. They lived in the same general area but they had very different beliefs about God.

This could describe much of today's world. The various religions often bring people into conflict with each other. Jesus too was surrounded by people who were opposed to him. But his message never changed. We need to stick to the simple truth of the Gospel message and learn to share it clearly and compassionately with anyone we meet, even our 'Samaria'.

Recently I was sitting on a public bench enjoying a relaxing break with my husband. Suddenly a young girl who was high on drugs came up to us and said, "You're in love, aren't you!" I told her that my husband and I were very happily married and had been for a long time. She proceeded to sit on my lap, wrap her arms around me like a little girl, and ask me questions about my personal life.

I could have been offended. I could have been afraid. She was a complete stranger and obviously incoherent. But before I could make the mistake of chucking her off my lap and storming away, I felt the Holy Spirit tug at my heart, as if to say, "There but for the grace of God, you would be just the same! Tell her I love her!"

At that moment of decision on my part, I remembered that I had a simple Christian witnessing tract in my purse. So I obeyed the tug of the Holy Spirit and asked this poor girl if I could give her something. She wanted my sunglasses, so I gave her those. And then I started reading her the little tract. It had a series of questions, which she answered as I read, until finally she grabbed the tract out of my hands and started reading it as loud as she could to me!

That was embarrassing! Even though I didn't know any of the other people who passed by, their expressions said it all. No one wanted to be caught dead with this girl! She was a mess!

But once I was a mess too! So were all of us before Jesus reached down and picked us up, forgave us, and give us his new life. I had a choice to make. Was I going to avoid this scary, hurting young 19-year-old girl or was I going to stick with her, in spite of her outward condition, and try to reach her heart. I decided to try and finish what God had started.

As we got to the end of the tract, I asked her if she believed what she had just read. She said, "YES!" And so I asked her if she wanted to give her heart to Jesus. Amazingly, she said "YES!" again. And as we began to pray, she started to change. She broke. The Gospel was the power she needed to accept Christ as her personal Saviour and begin a new life.

We need to reach out to our Samaria – no matter how scary they may seem. The great distinctive of Christianity is that the message of Jesus is a message of LOVE.

- "For God so loved the world that he gave his only begotten Son, that whoever believes in him should not perish but have everlasting life. For God did not send his Son into the world to condemn the world, but that the world through him might be saved." John 3:16-17

- "For the wages of sin is death, but the gift of God is eternal life through Jesus Christ our Lord." Romans 6:23

- "God demonstrates His own love for us, in that while we were yet sinners, Christ died for us." Romans 5:8

- "Beloved let us love one another, for love is of God, and everyone that loves is born of God and knows God." I John 4:7

Even scary people have the right to know who Jesus really is. Many think they know God, but without a personal relationship with Christ as Savior they cannot receive forgiveness that only he offers. Let love be our motivation, love for people and love for God when sharing with them.

THE ENDS OF THE EARTH: You may think that this phrase just applies to missionaries, Christians who are 'called' to leave their homeland and travel to a distant country to share their faith in Christ.

But in this modern age of jet travel, human migration and multiculturalism, the ends of the earth often live across the street or right next-door. And Jesus wants us to be a witness to them as well.

Once I lived in a tiny village in the Midlands, the central part of Great Britain. Now you would think that only white, English men and women lived in this rural farmland where coal burned in every home and the post office, newsagent, and village hall surrounded the small central green. It certainly LOOKED British on the outside.

But soon after we moved in there was a knock on my front door. When I opened it, a tall, young Asian woman pushed her pram and baby into my front hall, talking wildly in a foreign language. I had no idea who she was or what she wanted, but she was not leaving until she got her message across.

I found out that she was a Hindu, the wife of the owner of our village newsagent's, and she heard that I was a Christian. She wanted me to pray for her because of some very difficult situations in her personal life. I had the great privilege of leading her to Christ and she became one of my closest friends in that village.

My point is that you don't have to fly to the other side of the globe to reach the ends of the earth. Don't be afraid to respond to the needs of people from different cultures that live around you. For all their differences, they are people too. And people need the Lord!

Here is an example of the kind of prayer you can say as you lead someone to Christ. It is often referred to as the Sinner's Prayer. Practice saying it so that you can sincerely and personally share it with others.

"Heavenly Father, I now know that I need to be forgiven for all the sin and wrong in my life. I believe that you gave your Son Jesus to take my punishment and pay for all my sins. Thank you, Lord Jesus, for dying on the Cross for me. I accept you now as my Saviour, Lord and God. Thank you for giving me new life and a new future and for taking me home to be with you in heaven one day. Father, I praise you for accepting me into your family now in Jesus name. Amen!"

So, welcome to the family! The family of God is growing every day, all over the world. You are now a part of this great family and you have the privilege of welcoming others, as you become a witness in your own world.

DISCIPLINED LIVING

By Kenn Baird

We supposedly live in a modern age! But consider this - we may have taller buildings, but shorter tempers, wider freeways, but narrower viewpoints. We spend more, but we have less. We buy more, but enjoy it less.

We have bigger houses and smaller families, more conveniences and less time. We have more degrees but less common sense, more knowledge but less judgment, more experts but more problems, more medicine but poorer health.

We spend too recklessly, laugh too little, drive too fast, get too angry too quickly, stay up to late, get up too tired, read to seldom, watch TV too much and pray too little.

We have multiplied our possessions but reduced our values. We talk too much, love too seldom and lie too often.

We've learned how to make a living but not a life. We've added years to life but not more life to our years.

We've been all the way to the moon and back but have trouble crossing the street to meet the new neighbour.

We've conquered outer space but not inner space. We've done larger things but not better things. We've cleaned up the air but polluted the soul. We've split the atom but not our prejudice. We write more but learn less, plan more but accomplish less.

We've learned to rush but not to wait. We have higher incomes but lower morals, more food but our appetites are never satisfied, more acquaintances but fewer friends, more effort but less success.

We build more computers to hold more information, to produce more copies than ever but have less communication. We've become long on quantity but short on quality.

These are the times of fast food and slow digestion, tall men and short character, steep profits and shallow relationships.

These are the times of world peace but domestic warfare, more leisure and less fun, more kinds of food but less nutrition.

These are the days of two incomes but more divorce, of fancier houses but broken homes.

These are the days of quick trips, disposable nappies, throwaway morality, one-night stands, overweight bodies and pills that do everything from cheer to kill.

As someone once said, "We are living in a time when there is much in the shop window and nothing in the stockroom." The following story perfectly sums up the stupidity of the way we seek one thing and end up with another.

A newspaper reported that when a man attempted to steal petrol from a motor home vehicle parked on a street, he got much more than he bargained for. Police arrived at the scene to find a very sick man curled up next to the motor home near spilled sewage. A police spokesman said that the man admitted to trying to steal petrol and plugged his siphon hose into the motor home's sewage tank by mistake. The owner of the vehicle declined to press charges, saying that it was the best laugh he'd ever had.

We need wisdom to make a success out of life. Consider your job. Ask yourself, "Does God care about my job and where I work?" Now read 2 Timothy 2:15. Between the ages of 23-65 years, you will probably spend more time in your job than in any other life activity. That means you will effectively spend twice as much time with work colleagues as with family members. You will spend ten times more time there than with church members.

Now ask the question again. Of course God cares about your job. God meets you where you are and for most of us, that's in the work place. The workplace is the world's number one mission field. The workplace is the means of financial reward and God cares about your job because he cares about you, your witness and your finances.

Discipline in life is essential to success and it all starts with your thinking. In Numbers 13 we read of the account of the Hebrew spies that were sent into the land of Canaan to gather facts prior to the move into the land. Learning to give a good account is the first step in learning to live in victory. The spies were sent to:

1. Learn how to fight the victory, and

2. Learn the benefits that victory would bring.

It was never about whether they could or could not be victorious. They had been sent in knowing they would be victorious. (Read verses 1-26). Sadly, the story takes a negative turn at this point. The spies returned with a negative report, the very opposite of what they had been sent to do! They lost sight of their goal and focused on doubt. As a result, they brought a report of failure before even beginning.

Now read on into Numbers 14:7-9. Here we discover Joshua and Caleb. They brought a different report. They were 'in line' with God's plan and gave a report of life and victory.

We can learn important lessons through this story. When gathering facts, don't approach details as pitfalls and reasons to give up. View them as obstacles to be overcome. Tell the truth with faith and get a spiritual 'can do' attitude. Be an encourager and pray for God's answers to specific problems. Pray it before you say it and expect God to respond. Now read Hebrews 11:6 and Matthew 6:33. Put yourself into the place where you seek God first.

Learning to discipline the mind requires a 'double renewal' of heart and mind. God can only do heart renewal. Mind renewal involves you. The ten spies did not attempt to discipline their minds; they simply allowed their environment to make up their mind for them. Whereas Joshua and Caleb chose to focus on God's promise and tune out what the situation was saying to them. This is what takes discipline. Keeping your focus on God's word and limiting the influence of other outside influences.

Renewal of the heart means that you repent, are forgiven, confess Christ as Lord and thus are saved. But it was God who renewed your heart. You played a part but God did the renewing. It is a gift that cannot be earned and is completely undeserved. How amazing!

Now let's look at the renewal of the mind. The heart might be renewed at salvation but the mind continues to receive input from earthly, sensual, and even demonic sources throughout your life that will either enhance or impede your spirit.

Romans 12:1-2 encourages us to 'Prove what is good...'. This means discerning God's wisdom. Renewal brings about the ability to discern the wisdom of God in any situation or circumstance. Let's look at the words used here.

1. Conformed: This means to be "pressed into its mould."

2. Transformed: This means to "undergo a change" (Metamorphosed).

3. Prove what is good.

The purpose of the renewed mind is to discern God's wisdom and live effectively. So how do we do it? Turn to Ephesians 4:21-23 and note the three steps involved in renewing the mind.

1. Put off the Old.

2. Change the Mindset.

3. Put on the New.

Make sure you learn this formula: Put off / Change / Put On

Choose to renew your mind!

One of my great family holiday memories was the time we went gold panning in Cornwall. Up until that point I knew very little about gold. We panned away diligently for hours and only found a few small pieces of 'fools gold' which was absolutely worthless but the anticipation of a life-changing discovery was exhilarating.

Pure Gold has two remarkable characteristics that speak great spiritual truths to our hearts and minds. It is a softer, more malleable form of gold. Likewise we must develop a softness of heart that allows God to touch our conscience with a still small voice and not with a loud shout. Then he can easily mould us. Purest gold (liquid form) is transparent, fluid light - you can virtually see through the metal. We need a 'see through' me and 'see Jesus' quality to our lives.

As you leave this short chapter, listen carefully to the words God spoke to Joshua and discover just how relevant they are for you today. "Keep this book of the Law always on your lips; meditate on it day and night, so that you may be careful to do everything written in it. Then you will be prosperous and successful," (Joshua 1:8). Ask the Lord to help you discipline your heart and mind and enjoy your journey with Jesus.

GETTING INVOLVED

By Kenn Baird

One of the great tragedies of the nineteenth century was the career of Oscar Wilde. He had a brilliant mind and won the highest academic honours. He was a scintillating writer and won the highest awards in literature. He had all the charm in the world and was a man whose instinct it was to be kind, yet he fell to temptation and was imprisoned in disgrace.

When he was suffering for his fall, he wrote his book *De Profundis* and in it he said: *"The gods had given me almost everything. But I let myself be lured into long spells of senseless and sensual ease…. Tired of being on the heights I deliberately went to the depths in search for new sensation. What the paradox was to me in the sphere of thought, perversity became to me in the sphere of passion. I grew careless of the lives of others. I took pleasure where it pleased me and passed on. I forgot that every little action of the common day makes or unmakes character, and that therefore what one has done in the secret chamber, one has some day to cry aloud from the house-top. I ceased to be lord over myself. I was no longer the captain of my soul, and did not know it. I allowed pleasure to dominate me. I ended in horrible disgrace."*

The difference between success and failure is often the ability to get up just one more time than you fall down! Moses could easily have given up. The Bible heroes we read about were not superhuman characters. They were ordinary men and women just like you and me.

Consider Moses. He had what we might refer to in politically correct terms an 'interrupted' childhood. He was a foster child who lived with a foster family. He also had a temper, a speech impediment and a criminal record, but when God called to him, he ultimately said 'Yes'.

Then there was Joshua. He had seen the Promised Land and then had been forced to wander in the wilderness for forty years with people who didn't believe as he did. He then had to learn to conquer enemies and possess the land. He could have given up in discouragement, but he was willing to go when God said to 'Go'.

What about Peter? He had a hard time making the transition from fisherman to fisher of men. He nearly drowned while trying to walk on water, was strongly rebuked by Jesus for trying to tell him what to do, and denied knowing Jesus in that hour when Jesus needed him most. He could easily have seen himself as a hopeless failure. But when the opportunity came to preach the Gospel before thousands on the Day of Pentecost, Peter responded.

It really doesn't matter what you've done in the past or what mistakes you have made. God gives us a new opportunity to live a fulfilling future. He did this by forgiving us of our past and than giving us the Holy Spirit. Now we are empowered to live for others, serve others and make a difference in our world. And a good place to begin is in your local church. We're only failures if we lie down and give up.

Lets take a look at what type of things could potentially stop you from getting involved in serving others. Turn with me to Galatians 5:16-25. Here we learn that God not only intends for you to be free from the control of sin but that you start to walk according to the Spirit (Romans 8:4). The term 'walk' refers to your 'lifestyle'.

Now turn to Romans 8:1-17. There are three areas that we need to be very clear on if we want to effectively walk in the Spirit.

Firstly, verse 9 says you must learn to know who you are in Christ. This refers to your standing before God and not to your lifestyle. 'In the flesh' refers to being unsaved, 'in the spirit' refers to being 'saved and set free' (look at verse 1).

Secondly, in verse 5 we discover that being a follower of Jesus and living like one can be two very different things. Compare the difference between 1 Corinthians 3:1-3 and Ephesians 4:1.

Thirdly, in verse 5 you can see how your mindset and actions will give you away. You can reject what is in your heart and mind, but you can't live out what is not there. Galatians 5:3 informs us that salvation is not an opportunity for self indulgence but rather the source of power intended to develop us into becoming spiritual people.

Now read Titus 2:11-12, and 1 Peter 4:1-14. Thoughts can be tricky things! Romans 8:6 teaches us that to set our minds on the flesh is death but to set it on the spirit is life and peace. However, many followers of Jesus do not choose the life-style of the spirit until they have been cornered by the death-like experience of a 'flesh-led' life.

Now carefully read 2 Peter 1:3. This is a promise from God to you. His divine power (not your power) provides everything you need for your life and godliness (growing to be like Jesus), and it comes through your knowledge of him (relationship). Can you see why the devotional life is so important?

Romans 7:24 tells us that nothing good dwells in our flesh life. Verse 18 tells us that we cannot overcome sin without God's help. You can never walk in the Spirit until you understand the power of the old sinful nature and the futility of life apart from God (7:14-23). But make sure you understand that Paul is not in a hopeless depression here. He knows the resources of Jesus. Compare Romans 7:1-4 and Ephesians 3:16.

Falling into a trap can be easy to do. Traps are never obvious. By their very nature they are designed to entrap by stealth and cunning. Consider the following types of traps.

The Mouse Trap: This is a trap of deceit. The mouse sees only the cheese and fails to see the trap. The mouse enters the trap, tastes the cheese and snap! The mouse quickly discovers that the trap is stronger than he is. It is a fatal lesson for the mouse to learn. Beware of the snares of the enemy.

The Complacency Trap: We have a small pond in our garden and for many years we have resident frogs. Each year several other would-be frog parents arrive and we have a mass of tadpoles. As a result I have researched frogs and frog behaviour. For instance, did you know that a frog could filter out of its field of vision everything around it except food sources and danger? Now that's impressive. But a frog can also be incredibly stupid. If you were to place a frog (and please don't actually do this at home!) into a pan of luke-warm water, covering two thirds of the frog and increasing the heat by 0.5 degrees Fahrenheit every 5 minutes, the frog would sit there until it is completely cooked! There is nothing to stop the frog leaping out of the pan any time it chooses but because the change of temperature is so gradual it never seems urgent enough to act. Beware of complacency.

The Familiarity Trap: Some of the first settlers to the United States watched the native Indians float pumpkins downstream to where ducks were congregating. At first the ducks were startled and quickly flew away but after repeating this process over time and with great patience, the Indians found that the ducks were no longer startled and began to accept the floating pumpkins. Then the Indians hollowed out pumpkins and placed them on their heads. They started to slowly walk downstream with the other floating pumpkins and suddenly jump up out of the water and catch a duck. Beware of becoming familiar with things we no longer fear or avoid (drugs, pornography, alcohol, immorality, etc.).

The Tradition Trap: One species of processionary caterpillars travels nose to tail in a convoy to forage for food, then disperses to eat. After the meal they line up again, reforming the convoy to find more food. As part of an experiment in caterpillar behaviour, a biologist placed some caterpillars onto the rim of a flowerpot, nose to tail. Off they went following the leader (but there was no leader). They did this without ceasing for 3 days until they fell off exhausted. Beware of traditions that lead nowhere but will exhaust you nevertheless.

The Treasure Trap: A friend from Africa told me the story of how to catch a monkey by putting a banana in a jar. The monkey comes along and reaches into the jar, grabs hold of the banana but won't let go. It cannot remove both its hand and the banana and so it is trapped. Are you holding onto something you consider too good to give up? Beware of being trapped by what your eyes see.

And finally there is one more things to consider. I am often asked the question, "Why should I go to church?" My favourite answer lies in the following story. A man wrote a letter to the editor of a newspaper and complained that it made no sense to go to church every Sunday. "I've gone for 30 years now," he wrote, "and in that time I have heard something like 3,000 sermons. But for the life of me, I can't remember a single one of them. So, I think I'm wasting my time and the pastors are wasting theirs by giving sermons at all." This started a real controversy in the "Letters to the Editor" column, much to the delight of the editor. It went on for weeks until someone wrote this clincher:

"I've been married for 30 years now. In that time my wife has cooked some 32,000 meals. But, for the life of me, I cannot recall the entire menu for a single one of those meals. But I do know this. They all nourished me and gave me the strength I needed to do my work. If my wife had not given me these meals, I would be physically dead today. Likewise, if I had not gone to church for nourishment, I would be spiritually dead today!" Faith sees the invisible, believes the incredible and receives the impossible! Thank God for our physical AND spiritual nourishment!

We don't want to confuse going to church with serving the Lord. But from the former example we can see that going to church is necessary for spiritual growth, which then puts us in a place for serving in the church. Do something definite. Ask yourself this question: "What can I do to serve in this place?" Talk to the Pastor or leaders. Volunteer your services. Above all, ask the Lord to show you where you can serve. If we live dedicated lives of service to Christ, we have every right to expect God to supply the divine resources for the accomplishment of that service. God's fatherly heart can create a whole-hearted devotion in you and a love for those around you.

The greatest form of service is in 'Soul Winning', telling others about who Jesus is and helping them accept him as their personal Saviour. It is a command (Matthew 28:18-20). Jesus commands his followers to 'Go' and as you 'Go' to do certain things. Making Jesus' command a part of daily life is one of the highest acts of service in life.

Whatever your job is, there are three things Jesus wants you to make a part of your daily life. They are three commands rolled into one.

1) Make disciples -- Be a missionary to everyone you encounter.

2) Baptise them -- Bring to repentance, faith, and baptism.

3) Teach them -- Disciple a new believer and teach them to do likewise. Teach them what Jesus said and did and don't add your own version.

Are you ready to obey and serve? Now read Philippines 3:10. You are created to be a vessel of God's presence to pour out to others. God doesn't use you because you are smart, qualified or trained but because he empowers you to win souls.

Here is a typical imaginary conversation:

What are you living for? For my job.

Why? To make money.

Why? To pay bills and buy food.

Why? To eat, sleep and have a safe home.

Why? To have strength and health.

Why? So I can do my job.

Living to do your job is no longer your goal in life. As a Christian your reason for living is to claim the purposes of God, be filled with the Spirit and bring others to Christ. When this as your goal in life, God will add everything else you need.

Now read Matthew 6:33. We block the flow of the Spirit in our lives when we stop him from fulfilling his purposes. Read Matthew 20:28 and notice how Jesus did not have a 'me first' attitude.

We desperately need deliverance from the greatest 'ism' in the world.

It's not communism.

It's not Taoism.

It's not Hedonism.

But it is 'ME-ism'.

Read what the Apostle Paul writes in Philippians 1:21: "For me to live is Christ and to die is gain." We must learn to live for God and others as followers of Christ.

There are also many practical ways you can serve in the church (Romans 12:7). Prioritise your time to meet the needs of your brothers and sisters. Do you have practical skills that you could offer? Could you befriend a lonely person, help someone in the garden, offer to transport an elderly person, visit the housebound? Make a list of what you can do and ask God to show you opportunities for service.